FINDING THE ZODIAC KILLER

HOW I DECIPHERED THE IDENTITY OF
THE NATION'S MOST NOTORIOUS SERIAL KILLER

DAVID DANIEL

In the late 1960s and early 1970s, a serial killer who called himself the ZODIAC terrorized Northern California with cold-blooded murders and a series of taunting ciphers and letters. His first set of three ciphers, considered at the time to be one, were sent to three newspapers in 1969. They were cracked by a couple within a week. On July 11, 2021, David Daniel read where the Zodiac had stated in a letter that the three ciphers revealed his identity, but the couple and the authorities claimed that it wasn't there. David believed that the authorities had said the ciphers didn't reveal the Zodiac's identity for one reason—they couldn't find it. He knew it was there and he knew that he would find it. He looked at the first of the three ciphers—the one that the Zodiac had sent to the Vallejo Times Herald. Within three to seven seconds, he knew he had solved the nation's most notorious unsolved murder case. David studied the cipher further and looked at other ciphers that the killer had sent. One by one he cracked the ciphers and completely solved another. Within two minutes he had absolutely confirmed the secret identity of the ZODIAC killer multiple times. Law enforcement and cryptographers have been searching for his identity for over 50 years. Finally, the search is over. He has been found!

FINDING THE Z⊕DIAC KILLER

HOW I DECIPHERED THE IDENTITY OF
THE NATION'S MOST NOTORIOUS SERIAL KILLER

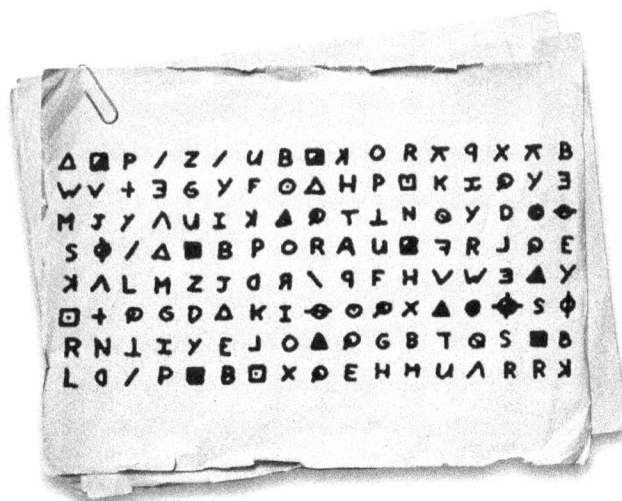

Library of Congress Control Number: 2023915065

PRINTED IN THE UNITED STATES OF AMERICA
FIRST PAPERBACK EDITION, 2023

Finding the Zodiac Killer
How I Deciphered The Identity Of The Nation's Most Notorious Serial Killer
DAVID DANIEL

EDITED BY BLYTHE DANIEL
ART AND PHOTO WORK BY DAVID RAPKA

1. Zodiac killer
2. Serial Killers
3. True Crime
4. Cold Cases
5. Cryptography
6. Codebreaking

RAJANATA PUBLISHING
3130 BALFOUR RD.
STE. D - 428
BRENTWOOD, CA 94513-5516

www.thecodebreaker.org
email: david@thecodebreaker.org

ISBN-13-979-8-218-25640-1

Books by David Daniel

The Mentalist Code
and the Search for Red John

Finding the Zodiac:
How I Deciphered the Identity of the
Nation's Most Notorious Serial Killer

The Code: The Secret Code Hidden
in the English Language

For the victims who weren't allowed to finish their lives or fulfill their dreams and for their families and friends and other loved ones who never got closure, I dedicate this book. When I read about the torture experienced by the victims, I was horrified. I was incensed by this killer's cruelty and by his taunts and because of this I was inspired to find the Zodiac's identity.

I also dedicate this book to all members of law enforcement who devoted their time and energy to solving this case and for doing their best to apprehend the killer. I have read about their work. I do not want all of their efforts to go for naught.

I dedicate this book to Robert Graysmith who spent hours and days and weeks and months and years searching for the Zodiac.

I further dedicate this book to Paul Avery and all of the other dedicated journalists who gave their time in pursuit of this killer.

It is for all of you that I have been inspired to bring closure to this case.

ACKNOWLEDGMENTS

With admiration and gratitude to:

Blythe Daniel for her superb editing skills

David Rapka for his outstanding artwork and photo work

My family whose support is immeasurable

TABLE OF CONTENTS

"The truth is always hidden
in plain sight"

David Daniel

CIPHER

*In cryptography, a cipher is an algorithm
for transforming a text to Ciphertext through encryption
or a Ciphertext to Plaintext through decryption*

INTRODUCTION

IN THE
WRONG PLACE
AT THE
RIGHT TIME

This book tells the story of the murders committed by the Zodiac Killer, his taunting of the police, press, and public, the 50-year search for his identity and, finally, the story of how I uncovered his identity.

It begins with a prologue—a story of some very strange encounters that I have had. They include my encounters with serial killers. I have met three. That is three more than most people have ever met and three more than most people would ever want to meet. You might say I was in the wrong place at the right time.

And I have met three people who have had encounters with serial killers. One of these encounters was safe enough, but the other two people I have met have had close ones. They were definitely in the wrong place—but at the right time. In both of these cases, they are very lucky to have survived.

On top of all this, I was there when law enforcement came to question an employee that resembled the 1985 sketch of a serial killer called the Night Stalker. Elsewhere, a friend's father painted their house out of fear that the color was too similar to houses invaded by the Night Stalker.

I have also made intelligent, educated guesses about serial killers. One was regarding the Hillside Stranglers being two men instead of one. Years later, I made an educated guess on the whereabouts of the Grim Sleeper's residence. I told people the Grim Sleeper lived near the corner of 81st and Western in Los Angeles, California. He did.

And I found the codes and clues that reveal the secret identity of *Red John*—a serial killer on the TV series *The Mentalist*. That is the subject of one of my books —*The Mentalist Code and the Search for Red John*.

Solving the identity of a fictional serial killer after just the first two episodes of *The Mentalist* was a lot of fun, as was continuing to watch for and follow up on codes and clues for several years throughout the series until the big reveal.

But solving the identity of a real serial killer has been a very different journey. It has meant reading about the horrific murders of real people and reading about the real taunts of the real public, the real police, and the real press by an authentic—not fictional—narcissistic psychopath. A monster with no regard for human life.

PROLOGUE

STRANGE
ENCOUNTERS

March 21, 1966
Quincy, Illinois

DONETTA KAY PICKENS

JUDITH ANN GREENING

The bodies of two young women, DONETTA KAY PICKENS, 21, and JUDITH ANN GREENING, 22, were found. Donetta had been found in the trunk of her own car. Both women had been stabbed multiple times. Judith had also been shot.

The two women had first gone missing on March 21, 1966. On March 22, neither of them showed up for work. This was highly suspicious because they were dependable at their jobs and always on time. A man was walking on South 24th Street when he discovered the body of Judith Ann Greening. Later that day, an off-duty police officer saw the car of Donetta Kay Pickens—her body was in the trunk. The horrendous murder caused a big disturbance in my hometown of Quincy, Illinois. Some people noted that the total number of stabbings of the two women added up to 66 which they believed to be intentional because the year was 1966. A few believed it to be on purpose because it was similar to the number of the beast—666. But most believed the total amount of stabbings to have no intentional meaning.

August, 1966
Quincy, Illinois

RONALD WILLIAM MCCLEERY GLAS

RONALD WILLIAM MCCLEERY GLAS, who had been arrested for the murders of the two women, was found not guilty of the murder of Donetta Kay Pickens. While things he had said to the police during interrogation may have led to a guilty verdict had they been allowed to be presented in court, nothing he had said to the police was admissible in his trial. This was because of the then-recent Miranda case and, therefore, he would not be tried for the murder of Judith Ann Greening.

Ronald was often seen walking to a particular gas station for soda in Quincy, Illinois. One day, on a dare from a friend, I approached him and said, "Hey, you got away with it. You really put one over on them bozos, didn't you?" He looked sort of surprised by someone suddenly questioning him right up in his face, but after a few seconds, he looked proud in reaction to my apparent admiration. "Yeah, I got away with it. I showed them!" I considered his response to be a possible admission of guilt, but an authority told me it was not.

In 1989, RONALD WILLIAM MCCLEERY GLAS was arrested for the murder of Mary Ann (DeCrevel) Kuster, 42, and he was convicted of her murder. He had stabbed her multiple times and had left her body in the trunk of her own car just like he had likely done to Donetta Kay Pickens. If he committed at least three murders, and it appears he did, the third murder being distant in time from the other two murders qualifies Glas as a serial killer. That is not to say that by using this definition he is comparable to the kind of serial killers for whom killing is a compulsion or an addiction like it was for killers like JOHN WAYNE GACY and THEODORE ROBERT BUNDY.

April, 1977
Quincy, Illinois

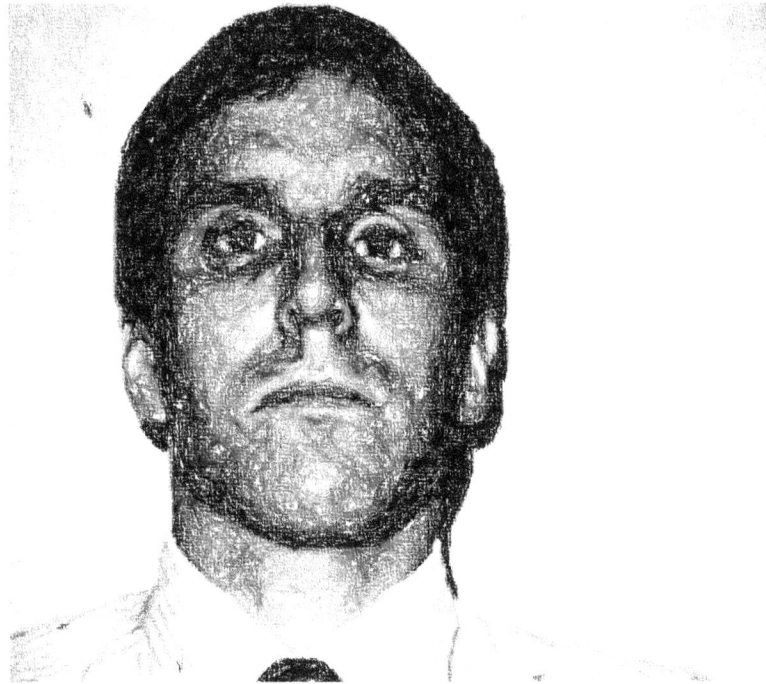

JOSEPH MICHAEL SWANGO

JOSEPH MICHAEL SWANGO, known as MICHAEL SWANGO, had been the valedictorian of his class at Catholic Boys High School in Quincy, Illinois. In Quincy, just about every grade school had an outside basketball court on its grounds, and guys would gather when school was not in session to play some basketball. I was taking my vacation in my hometown of Quincy. This particular day was the second day in a row I was playing basketball with mostly the same bunch–that included Michael Swango. After the game we played Horse. I was better at this game than I was at basketball. I had several tricks I had practiced, including bouncing the ball into the basket and throwing the ball over my head backwards. After the game, Michael and I walked a couple of blocks. There was a store nearby, so we went in for a soda.

He asked me, "Do you ever wonder what happens to people when they die?"

I replied, "Some people say we go to Heaven or Hell, while others think we reincarnate."

I didn't give him a chance to respond. I quickly asked him, "What do you think?"

He said, "I don't mean where we go. I mean—what happens when someone dies?"

He suddenly looked somewhat demented to me.

Swango would go on to be awarded his medical license but was not invited to stay on for a neurosurgery residency.

In 1985, while working as a paramedic in Quincy, Illinois, he was arrested for poisoning his co-workers. This was quite shocking to me.

In 1997, Dr. Swango was arrested for multiple murders of patients in hospitals, and he became known as a serial killer who was soon nicknamed the Doctor of Death. He is believed to have poisoned to death as many as 60 patients and colleagues, but he only confessed to four.

He was convicted of murder in 2000 and was sentenced to three consecutive life terms with no possibility of parole.

The next day, as fate would have it, I took a bus from Quincy to a bus station in Des Plaines, Illinois.

April, 1977
Des Plaines, Illinois

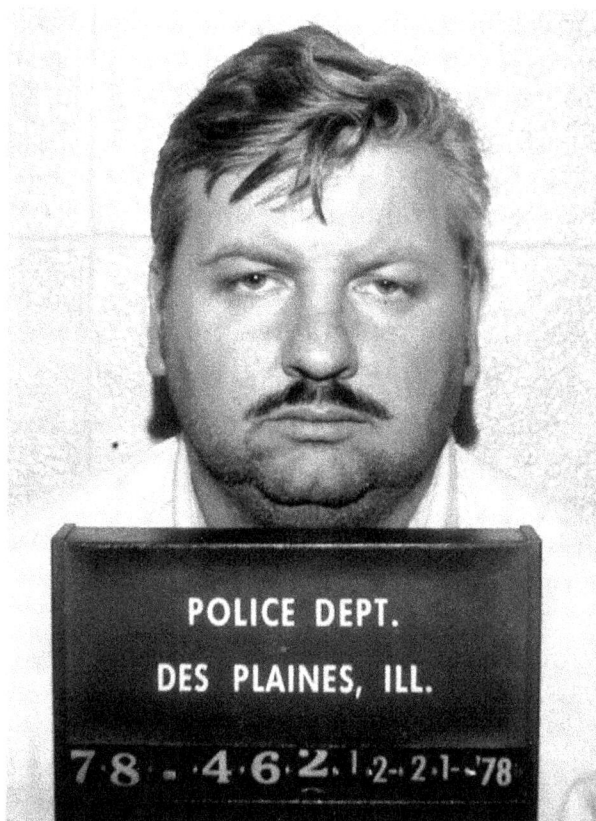

JOHN WAYNE GACY

I arrived at the Des Plaines Greyhound Bus Station (which, by the way, no longer exists). It was the closest bus station to Hoffman Estates where my family lived, and I was coming for my annual visit from California. I used a pay phone to call to see if my dad was home and if he could come pick me up. I was in luck and I mean —very much in luck because he was home to answer the phone. He said, "Sure, I'm on my way." Then, I walked outside, and I set down my bags.

A man—plump, about 5 foot 9 inches tall with greying hair—sitting in his car— asked me,

"Would you like a ride?"

I told him, "No thanks."

He said, "I'll give you a ride anywhere you want to go."

I repeated, "No thanks."

We were surrounded by nearly a dozen people who were watching and listening to our conversation as this man was trying to get me in his car.

"I have marijuana."

"No thanks. My dad is picking me up."

"We could smoke some marijuana until your dad gets here."

I noticed that an older couple was looking back and forth at the man and me each time we spoke.

"Do you need a job?"

I knew that he wasn't going to stop, so I went inside the bus station to wait—all the while peeking outside to watch for my dad.

Finally, my dad arrived. As I walked toward my dad's car, I looked around and I saw that the man was parked a little more distant--waiting to see if my dad was really picking me up. I must admit—the man was really creepy and scary.

December 1978
Chicago, Illinois

There was news of a man near Des Plaines, Illinois, named JOHN WAYNE GACY. Law enforcement had dug up multiple bodies of young males in his yard. The story became a major news item.

Late 1978/Early 1979
Los Angeles, California

I read about JOHN WAYNE GACY in a magazine. I remember when I first saw and stared at his picture. It was the man who had offered me a ride at the bus station. I was in shock. I called and told a few people, including my parents, that this man had offered me a ride at the Des Plaines bus station.

Previously, I stated that there were times when I have been 'in the wrong place at the right time.' This was one of those times. I was in the wrong place—being within a few yards of Gacy with him asking me if he could give me a ride. It was at the right time because my dad answered the phone and he was going to come pick me up.

15

If he had not been home, I would have walked out of the bus station and walked to a place where I could hitchhike. Not most likely—but most certainly—Gacy would have driven over to pick me up and I would not be here today.

Just as I turned him down, I can be sure that others turned him down, as well. He wasn't waiting for time to pass for him to need or seek another victim. The time that passed between the dates of his murders was because of the fact that boys and young men were saying, "No."

He murdered at least 34 males, if we include Charles Antonio Hattula who was strongly considered to be a victim by investigators as (1) he was Gacy's employee (2) they had been involved in conflicts, and (3) it would explain an inaccuracy in Gacy's confession about how many boys he threw into rivers.

In a phone interview I had with Des Plaines police detective Rafael Tovar in 1998, he told me that when he asked how many people he had killed, Gacy's exact words were, "I always liked the number 45!"

December 1977
Los Angeles, California

A serial killer was on the loose who was dubbed the Hillside Strangler. I called a young lady I had recently met at a club to ask if she would like to go see *Close Encounters of the Third Kind*. She said, "Yes." But she also told me that her parents had asked her, "How do you know this guy isn't the Hillside Strangler?" We both found this a bit amusing, but I acknowledged that her parents had reasons to worry about their daughter during a time like this.

I told a few people at that time that I believed the Hillside Strangler was two men— not one. And I added that one was likely a bit older than the other and they were stepbrothers or cousins. As it turns out, one was Kenneth Bianchi and the other was Angelo Buono and yes, they were cousins.

Late 1985/Early 1986
Burbank, California

I was sitting on a movie set, and someone brought up John Wayne Gacy for some reason. I told them about my being offered a ride by Gacy, himself. A woman at the next table got my attention and shared that she was used as bait to try to capture the Hillside Stranglers. She told me that she had called the police to tell them she was worried about a man she had just met who wanted her to meet his brother. This led to a detective telling her to call a phone number if he ever came to her home. One day, the man she had met and the man she assumed was his brother showed up at her door. She didn't answer it—she called the number she had been given. In just minutes, the neighborhood was inundated with police cars. Soon, the detective arrived and entered her home surrounded by police in uniform. Given the response she received from her call, she bluntly asked the detective if he thought these guys were the Hillside Stranglers. The sudden silence of all the officers told her the answer. She expressed her upset at being used as 'bait.'

Just as I had been in the wrong place at the right time with Gacy, this young lady had been in the wrong place at the right time. She was in the wrong place with Kenneth Bianchi and Angelo Bono knocking at her front door. The only thing that made this the right time for this to happen is that she did not answer the door because she had been warned and she had called the police.

September 1985
Los Angeles, California

At my place of work where I was a supervisor, the police came and picked up an employee and took him in to question him and to get his fingerprints. Several people who had seen the sketch of a serial killer called the Night Stalker in the Los Angeles Times had called the police to inform them about a young man who looked like the Night Stalker. The following day, the employee returned to work and told us why he had been taken in. He told us that he had been cleared.

Not far away from where I lived, a friend of mine told me that his father suddenly decided to paint their house. Their house was off a freeway—as were the homes of the Night Stalker's victims. It just so happened that the color of their house looked similar to homes of the Night Stalker's victims. My friend's family felt a little safer with their home painted a different color.

Spring 2000
Los Angeles, California

In a conversation with several people, I shared about my close encounter with John Wayne Gacy. A man named Harold Eugene Tate told us that he was the last near-victim of the serial killer, William Bonin, who was better known as the Freeway Killer. Tate had not volunteered for the job of bait. Undercover police had been tailing Bonin for some time as he unsuccessfully tried to get five other young males into his car. When Bonin picked up Harold Eugene Tate and parked his car, the police got near enough to the car to hear muffled screams for help and banging. At this point, they entered the van just in time to save Harold Tate's life.

Harold was truly in the wrong place at just the right time. Being handcuffed and tied up, Harold just knew he was about to die. The only way this was the right time for this to happen was because the plain clothes police officers broke into William Bonin's van just in time.

2002
Los Angeles, California

I was at the college where I taught, and I noticed that there were people there making a movie. They asked if I had the key to a room they needed to use. Coincidentally—as it turned out—the movie they were making was *Ted Bundy* (2002) which was a horror thriller film about the serial killer.

Early 2000s
Los Angeles, California

I began to record music with a very talented musician named David Vasquez. One day I brought up my experience with John Gacy. He told me that his father had been a barber and that he cut the hair of Angelo Buono, one of the Hillside Stranglers. In addition, the Buono's upholstery shop had been right across from the barber shop, and my friend had once gone there for an estimate. My friend's father—the barber—had also been interviewed for the news on TV. He said that he did not believe that Buono could do such a thing.

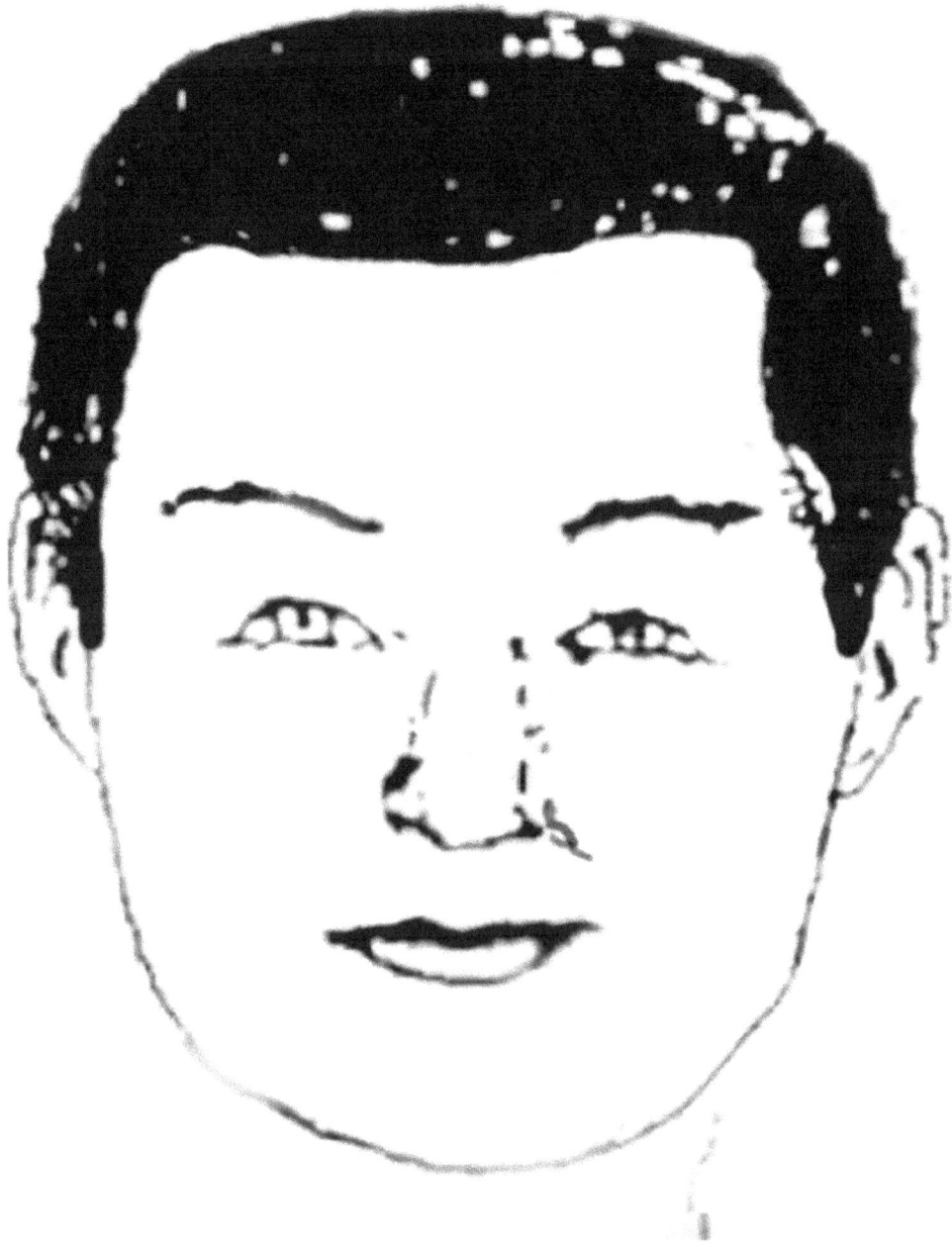

A
REIGN
OF
TERROR

In the late 1960s and early 1970s, the Zodiac Killer terrorized Northern California with cold-blooded murders and a series of taunting letters and ciphers.

In this section, you will read about the canonical five fatal victims attributed to the Zodiac and two other murder victims suspected to have been victims of the Zodiac.

I present all of the Zodiac's known ciphers. I also present all of the clues sent by the Zodiac that I have personally solved. I do not include clues that were found by others. One clue I found was also found by another author and by many others. I include this clue because I discovered it independently as did many.

December 20, 1968
Benicia, California

DAVID ARTHUR FARADY   **BETTY LOU JENSEN**

Two teenagers, DAVID ARTHUR FARADAY, 17, and BETTY LOU JENSEN, 16, were shot and killed on Lake Herman Road within the city limits of Benicia in the San Francisco Bay Area.

It is said they were on their first date and that they planned to attend a concert. They pulled over on Lake Herman Road, which was known as a 'Lovers Lane.' It is thought that the killer pulled up in a car next to them—ordering David to get out of the car. Then he shot both of them.

They were the first two victims that law enforcement feel certain were murdered by the Zodiac Killer.

July 4, 1969
Vallejo, California

DARLENE ELIZABETH FERRIN

DARLENE ELIZABETH FERRIN, 22, and MICHAEL RENAULT MAGEAU, 19, were shot in the parking lot of Blue Rock Springs Park in Vallejo, California. While Mageau survived the attack, Darlene Elizabeth Ferrin was pronounced dead on arrival at Kaiser Foundation Hospital. She is considered by authorities to be the third 'known' fatal victim of the Zodiac Killer.

August 1, 1969
Vallejo and San Francisco, California

The offices of three newspapers, the Vallejo Times Herald, the San Francisco Examiner, and the San Francisco Chronicle, receives letters and ciphers from a man claiming to have committed several recent murders in the area of Vallejo and San Francisco. The ciphers were treated as one cipher—which the killer said would reveal his identity.

This is the letter that the Zodiac sent to the Vallejo Times Herald

I am the killer of the 2 teenagers last Christmass at Lake Herman and the Girl last 4th of July. To Prove this I shall state some facts which only I & the police know
Christmass
Brand name of ammo Super X
10 Shots fired
Boy was on back feet to car
Girl was lyeing on right side feet to west
4th of July
Girl was wearing patterned Pants
Boy was also shot in knee
Brand name of ammo was Western
Here is a cyipher or that is part of one. the other 2 parts have been mailed to the S.F. Examiner & the S.F. Chronicle
I want you to print this cipher on your frunt page by Fry Afternoon Aug 1-69, If you do not do this I will go on a kill ram-page Fry night that will last the whole week end. I will cruse around and pick of all stray people or coupples that are alone then move on to kill some more untill I have killed over a dozen people.

This is the cipher that the Zodiac sent to the Vallejo Times Herald. It is most commonly known as the first part of the Z-408 Cipher, but it will be referred to by this author as the Z-136-A or the "Times Herald Cipher."

(The original breaking of this cipher will be discussed shortly. The complete solution was discovered later by this author).

Dear Editor

I am the killer of the 2 teenagers last Christmass at Lake Herman & the girl last 4th of July. To prove this I shall state some facts which only I & the police know.

Christmass

1. brand name of ammo - Super X
2. 10 shots fired
3. Boy was on his back with feet to car
4. Girl was lyeing on right side feet to west

4th of July

1. girl was wearing patterned pants
2. boy was also shot in knee
3. ammo was made by Western

Here is a cipher or that is part of one. The other 2 parts are being mailed to the Vallejo Times & S.F. Chronicle

I want you to print this cipher on the frunt page by Fry afternoon Aug 1-69. If you do not print this cipher, I will go on a kill rampage Fry night. This will last the whole weekend, I will cruse around killing people who are alone at night untill Sun Night or untill I kill a dozen people.

⊕

```
⊃ z K ⊘ ٩ I ⊕ W ⊘ I ▲ ● L ⋈ Я ⊿ ■
B P D R ✚ τ ⊼ ○ ⟍ N ◆ Ǝ E U H ⋋ F
Z ⊃ ٩ O V W I ● ✚ ⊥ L ⊖ ⌐ Λ R ⊖ H
I ⊿ D R □ T Y Я ⟍ ◁ Ǝ / ⊡ X ꓩ ◍ A
P ● ⋈ ▲ R U ⊥ ⊡ L ⊕ N V E K H ⊼ 6
Я I I ꓩ ⋋ ● ⊿ ▲ L ⋈ J N A ⊕ z φ P
◆ U ٩ ⋋ A ⊿ ■ B ⌄ W ⟍ ✚ V T ⊥ O P
Λ ⊼ S Я ⌐ ⊐ U Ǝ ⊙ ⊿ D ◆ G ■ ◨ I ⋈
```

This is the cipher that the Zodiac sent to the San Francisco Examiner. It is most commonly known as the second part of the Z-408 Cipher, but it will be referred to by this author as the Z-136-B or the "Examiner Cipher."

(The original breaking of this cipher will be discussed shortly. The complete solution was discovered later by this author).

This is the letter that the Zodiac sent to the San Francisco Chronicle

---

This is the murderer of the 2 teenagers last Christmass at Lake Herman & the girl on the 4th of July near the golf course in Vallejo

To prove I killed them I shall state some facts which only I & the police know.

Christmass

    1. Brande name of ammo Super X

    2. 10 shots were fired

the Dear Editor

    1. This boy was on his back with his feet to the car

    2. the girl was on her right side feet to the west

4th July

    1. girl was wearing paterned slacks

    2. The boy was also shot in the knee.

    3. Brand name of ammo was western

Over

Here is part of a cipher the other 2 parts of this cipher are being mailed to the editors of the Vallejo Times & SF Examiner.

I want you to print this cipher on the front page of your paper. In this cipher is my idenity.

If you do not print this cipher by the afternoon of Fry. 1st of Aug 69, I will go on a kill rampage Fry. night. I will cruse around all weekend killing lone people in the night then move on to kill again, untill I end up with a dozen people over the weekend.

This is the cipher that the Zodiac sent to the San Francisco Chronicle. It is most commonly known as the third part of the Z-408 Cipher, but it will be referred to by this author as the Z-136-C or the "Chronicle Cipher."

(The original breaking of this cipher will be discussed shortly. The complete solution was discovered later by this author).

August 4, 1969
San Francisco, California

The killer sent another letter to the San Francisco Examiner to 'prove' that he is the killer. With the recent ciphers still not solved even in part, the killer identifies himself as the Zodiac Killer by introducing himself, "This is the Zodiac speaking."

Dear Editor

This is the Zodiac speaking

In answer to your asking for more details about the good times I have had in Vallejo, I shall be very happy to supply even more material. By the way, are the police haveing a good time with the code? If not, tell them to cheer up; when they do crack it they will have me.

On the 4th of July:

I did not open the car door. The window was rolled down all ready. The boy was origionaly sitting in the front seat when I began fireing. When I fired the first shot at his head, he leaped backwards at the same time thus spoiling my aim. He ended up on the back seat then the floor in back thashing out very violently with his legs; thats how I shot him in the knee. I did not leave the cene of the killing with squealling tires & raceing engine as described in the Vallejo paper,. I drove away quite slowly so as not to draw attention to my car.

The man who told the police that my car was brown was a negro about 40–45 rather shabbly dressed. I was at this phone booth haveing some fun with the Vallejo cops when he was walking by. When I hung the phone up the dam X@ thing began to ring & that drew his attention to me & my car.

Last Christmass

In that epasode the police were wondering as to how I could shoot & hit my victoms in the dark. They did not openly state this, but implied this by saying it was a well lit night & I could see the silowets on the horizon. Bull Shit that area is srounded by high hills & trees. What I did was tape a small pencel flash light to the barrel of my gun. If you notice, in the center of the beam of light if you aim it at a wall or celling you will see a black or darck spot in the center of the circle of light about 3 to 6 inches across. When taped to a gun barrel, the bullet will strike exactly in the center of the black dot in the light. All I had to do was spray them as if it was a water hose; there was no need to use the gun sights. I was not happy to see that I did not get front page coverage.

⊕

August 8, 1969
Salinas, California

BETTYE AND DONALD HARDEN of Salinas, California cracked the 408-symbol cipher known as the Z-408, which contained a mix of characters and letters. In the cipher was an oft-misspelled letter in which the killer seemed to reference "The Most Dangerous Game," a 1924 short story written by Richard Connell about a big game hunter who falls from his yacht to find himself hunted by another big game hunter. The Zodiac also said that he was killing people because they would be his slaves in the afterlife. The couple were able to decipher the letter, but they stated that they could not find the identity of the killer—now known as the Zodiac Killer—in the cipher. The full solution was discovered later by David Daniel.

August 10, 1969
San Francisco, California

A letter that was postmarked in San Francisco on August 10, 1969, is sent to Vallejo Police Sergeant JOHN LYNCH. This was just two days after the San Francisco Chronicle published an article on Donald and Bettye Harden's codebreaking of the cipher. The article mentioned Sergeant John Lynch as being in charge of the investigation. This letter went unpublished and has been left out of much of what has been written about the Zodiac Killer. Perhaps, early on, the letter's authenticity was questioned, as the tone of the letter was in complete contradiction to the tone and personality of other letters sent by the Zodiac. And the letter was typed instead of handprinted. It was signed 'Concerned Citizen.' This was the first "Citizen" letter. A second that was signed 'Good Citizen' was sent on October 7, 1969. A third "Citizen" letter will also be shown in this book.

This is the first of three "Citizen" letters

Dear Sergeant Lynch,

I hope the enclosed "key" will prove to be beneficial to you in connection with the cipher letter writer.

Working puzzles criptograms and word puzzle is one of my pleasure. Please forgive the absence of my signature or name as I do not wish to have my name in the papers and it could be mentioned at the slip of the tongue

With best wishes,

Concerned citizen

(The clue of the "Citizen" letters has been solved by this author).

September 27, 1969
Napa County, California

CECILIA ANN SHEPARD

CECELIA ANN SHEPARD, 22, and BRYAN CALVIN HARTNELL, 20, were stabbed at Lake Berryessa in Napa County, California. Hartnell survived eight stab wounds to the back, but Cecilia Ann Shepard died as a result of her injuries on September 29, 1969.

She is the fourth fatal victim of the Zodiac according to a consensus by law enforcement.

This note was left on Bryan Hartnell's car who survived an attack by the Zodiac

⊕

Vallejo
12-20-68
7-4-69
Sept 27-69-6:30
By knife

Also, on September 27, 1969

Sketch taken from a female witness at Lake Berryessa

The first composite sketch of a suspect was made by ROBERT MCKENZIE from witnesses who had seen a suspicious male at Berryessa Park the day of the stabbings.

October 7, 1969
San Francisco, California

With no response to the earlier "Concerned Citizen" letter, the killer sends a second "Citizen" letter—the "Good Citizen" letter. It also goes unpublished and was considered questionable as to whether it was the work of the Zodiac until now.

(This is the aforementioned second "Citizen" letter—a clue that is later solved by this author). The "Good Citizen" letter is not available).

October 11, 1969
San Francisco, California

PAUL LEE STINE

PAUL LEE STINE, 29, a cab driver, is shot and killed in the Presidio Heights neighborhood in San Francisco. Paul Stine is the fifth of the canonical five—the five people to have been confirmed victims of the Zodiac by a consensus of law enforcement agencies and authorities.

October 13, 1969
San Francisco, California

The San Francisco Chronicle receives a letter from the Zodiac Killer in which the killer takes credit for the murder of Paul Stine.

This is the Zodiac speaking

I am the murderer of the taxi driver over by Washington St & Maple St last night, to prove this here is a bloodstained piece of his shirt. I am the same man who did in the people in the north bay area.

The S.F. Police could have caught me last night if they had searched the park properly instead of holding road races with their motorcicles seeing who could make the most noise. The car drivers should have just parked their cars and sat there quietly waiting for me to come out of cover.

School children make nice targets, I think I shall wipe out a school bus some morning. Just shoot out the front tire & then pick off the kiddies as they come bouncing out.

November 8, 1969
San Francisco, California

The San Francisco Chronicle receives the "Dripping Pen" letter and a new cipher from the Zodiac Killer. In the envelope is another cipher known as the Z-340 Cipher.

This is the Zodiac speaking

I though you would need a good laugh before you hear the bad news. You won't get the news for a while yet. *and i can't do a thing with it!*

PS could you print this new cipher on your frunt page? I get awfully lonely when I am ignored, so lonely I could do my Thing!!!!!!

⊕

Des July Aug Sept Oct = 7

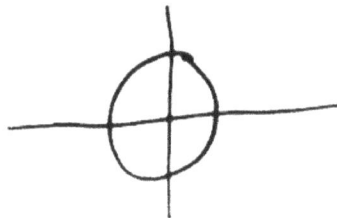

(The Z-340 Cipher was cracked in December 2020. The name of the Zodiac was found in the cipher in 2021 by this author).

April 20, 1970
San Francisco, California

The San Francisco Chronicle receives the "My Name Is..." Cipher that is now widely known as the Z-13 Cipher, and a Bomb Diagram.

This is the Zodiac speaking

By the way have you cracked the last cipher I sent you?

My name is

A E N ⊕ ⊗ K ⊗ M ⊗ ⊥ N A M

I am mildly cerous as to how much money you have on my head now. I hope you do not think that I was the one who wiped out that blue meannie with a bomb at the cop station. Even though I talked about killing school children with one. It just wouldn't doo to move in on someone elses teritory. But there is more glory in killing a cop than a cid because a cop can shoot back. I have killed ten people to date. It would have been a lot more except that my bus bomb was a dud. I was swamped out by the rain we had a while back.

The new bomb is set up like this

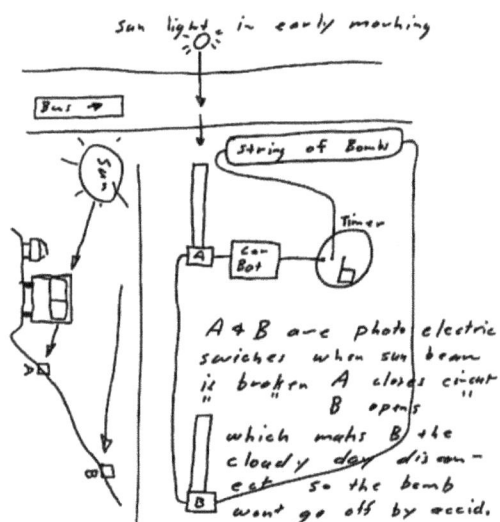

Sun light in early morning

Bus ➔

String of Bombs

Timer

Con-Bot

A + B are photo electric swiches when sun beam is broken A closes circut B opens which makes B the cloudy day discon- est so the bomb won't go off by accid.

PS I hope you have fun trying to figgure out who I killed

⊕ =10   sfpd = 0

(This cipher remained unsolved until this author solved it in 2021).

April 28, 1970
San Francisco, California

The San Francisco Chronicle receives the "Dragon Card"

If you don't want me to have this blast you must do two things. 1 Tell everyone about the bus bomb with all the details. 2 I would like to see some nice Zodiac butons wandering about town. Every one else has these buttons like, ☮, black power, melvin eats bluber, etc. Well it would cheer me up considerably if I saw a lot of people wearing my buton. Please no nasty ones like melvin's

Thank you

⊕

June 26, 1970
San Francisco, California

The San Francisco Chronicle receives the "Button" letter with a cipher

---

This is the Zodiac speaking.

I have become very upset with the people of San Fran Bay Area. They have <u>not</u> complied with my wishes for them to wear some nice ✢ buttons. I promiced to punish them if they did not comply, by anilating a full School Buss. But now school is out for the summer, so I punished them in another way. I shot a man sitting in a parked car with a .38.

✢-12

SFPD-0

The map coupled with this code will tell you where the bomb is set. You have untill next Fall to dig it up. ✢

C △ ⨯ | ■ O ⅄ ⅃ A M ⅂ ▲ Ω O R T ⊙
X ⊙ F D V ℧ ◨ H C Ɛ L ✢ P W △

(This cipher has never been solved).

July 24, 1970
San Francisco, California

The San Francisco Chronicle receives the "Kathleen Johns" letter

This is the Zodiac speaking

I am rather unhappy because you people will not wear some nice ⊕ buttons. So I now have a little list, starting with the woeman ✚ her baby that I gave a rather intersting ride for a couple howers one evening a few months back that ended in my burning her car where I found them.

⊕

July 26, 1970
San Francisco, California

The San Francisco Chronicle receives the "Little List" letter

This is the Zodiac speaking

Being that you will not wear some nice ✦ buttons, how about wearing some nasty ✦ buttons. Or any type of ✦ buttons that you can think up. If you do not wear any type of ✦ buttons, I shall (on top of everything else) torture all 13 of my slaves that I have wateing for me in Paradice. Some I shall tie over ant hills and watch them scream & twich and sqwirm. Others shall have pine splinters driven under their nails & then burned. Others shall be placed in cages & fed salt beef untill they are gorged then I shall listen to their pleass for water and I shall laugh at them. Others will hang by their thumbs & burn in the sun then I will rub them down with deep heat to warm them up. Others I shall skin them alive & let them run around screaming. And all billiard players I shall have them play in a darkened dungen cell with crooked cues & Twisted Shoes. Yes I shall have great fun inflicting the most delicious of pain to my slaves SFPD=0 ✦ =13

As some day it may hapen that a victom must be found. I've got a little list. I've got a little list, of society offenders who might well be underground who would never be missed who would never be missed. There is the pestulentual nucences who whrite for autographs, all people who have flabby hands and irritating laughs. All children who are up in dates and implore you with im platt. All people who are shakeing hands shake hands like that. And all third persons who with unspoiling take thoes who insist. They'd none of them be missed. They'd none of them be missed. There's the banjo seranader and the others of his race and the piano orginast I got him on the list. All people who eat pepermint and phomphit in your face, they would never be missed They would never be missed

42

And the Idiout who phraises with inthusastic tone of centuries but this and every country but his own. And the lady from the provences who dress like a guy who doesn't cry and the singurly abnormily the girl who never kissed. I don't think she would be missed Im shure she wouldn't be missed. And that nice impriest that is rather rife the judicial hummerest I've got him on the list All funny fellows, commic men and clowns of private life. They'd none of them be missed. They'd none of them be missed. And uncompromiseing kind such as wachmacallit, thingmebob, and like wise, well—nevermind, and tut tut tut tut, and whatshisname, and you know who, but the task of filling up the blanks I rather leave up to you. But it really doesn't matter whom you place upon the list, for none of them be missed, none of them be missed.

⊕

PS. The Mt. Diablo Code concerns Radians & # inches along the radians

September 6, 1970
South Lake Tahoe, California

DONNA ANN LASS

On September 6, 1970, DONNA ANN LASS, 25, disappeared. She had been working as a nurse in the first aid room at the Sahara Tahoe Hotel and Casino in Borderline, Nevada. Apparently sometime between 1:15 a.m., when she last logged in and 1:45 a.m., when she was expected to make another log in—she disappeared. She was from the San Francisco area but had recently moved to Borderline, Nevada.

The day after Donna Ann Lass disappeared, a man called her landlord and place of work to say she would be gone for a while due to a family emergency.

October 5, 1970
San Francisco, California

This postcard is suspected to be from the Zodiac

Mon. Oct 5, 1970

DEAR EDITOR

YOU'LL HATE ME BUT I'VE GOT TO TELL YOU
THE PACE ISN'T ANY
SLOWER! IN   'Some of Them
FACT IT'S JUST ONE BIG   13   Fought
Thirteenth   It Was Horrible"

THERE ARE REPORTS city police pig cops are closeing in on me. Fk I'm crackproof, What is the price tag now?

October 27, 1970
San Francisco, California

Paul Avery of the San Francisco Chronicle receives the "Halloween" letter

(This was a clue that the Zodiac sent in place of a cipher—but for the same purpose, which was to reveal his identity).

March 13, 1971
San Francisco, California

The Los Angeles Times receives the "Los Angeles Times'' letter. The Zodiac comments on the police's acknowledging the possibility of the Riverside murder of Cheri Josephine Bates. He could be taking credit for a murder he committed or he could be taking credit for a murder he did not commit. It is also worth mentioning that he is using the term "Blue Meanies" from the Beatles film, *Yellow Submarine*.

The Los Angeles Times receives the "Los Angeles Times'' letter

This is the Zodiac speaking

Like I have allways said, I am crack proof. If the Blue Meannies are evere going to catch me, they had best get off their fat asses & do something. Because the longer they fiddle & fart around, the more slaves I will collect for my after life. I do have to give them credit for stumbling across my riverside activity, but they are only finding the easy ones, there are a hell of a lot more down there. The reason I'm writing to the Times is this, They don't bury me on the back pages like some of the others.

SFPD-0

January 29, 1974
San Francisco, California

The San Francisco Chronicle receives the "Exorcist" letter

I saw and think "The Exorcist" was the best saterical comidy that I have ever seen.

Signed, yours truley:

He plunged himself into the billowy wave
and an echo arose from the suicide's grave
titwillo titwillo titwillo

PS. If I do not see this note in your paper, I will do something nasty, which you know I'm capable of doing.

February 14, 1974
San Francisco, California

The San Francisco Chronicle receives the "SLA" letter

Dear Mr. Editor,

Did you know that the initials SLAY (Symbionese Liberation Army) spell "sla," an old Norse word meaning "kill."

a friend

April 27, 1974
Las Vegas, Nevada

DANA MARIE LULL

DANA MARIE LULL, 15, was kidnapped in view of her boyfriend ROY NORMAN TOPHIGH. Her body was later found in a mine shaft on Mountain Springs Road in San Bernardino, California.

May 8, 1974
San Francisco, California

The San Francisco Chronicle receives the "Citizen Card" letter. It is signed 'a Citizen.' The letter is not connected in the media to the still unpublished "Concerned Citizen" and "Good Citizen" letters, and the clue continues to be largely unnoticed. This is the third "Citizen" letter written by the Zodiac.

The San Francisco Chronicle receives the "Citizen Card" letter

Sirs—I would like to express my consternation concerning your poor taste & lack of sympathy for the public, as evidenced by your running of the ads for the movie "Badlands," featuring the blurb—"In 1959 most people were killing time. Kit & Holly were killing people." In light of recent events, this kind of murder-glorification can only be deplorable at best (not that glorification of violence was ever justifiable) why don't you show some concern for public sensibilities & cut the ad?

A citizen

July 8, 1974
San Francisco, California

The San Francisco Chronicle receives the "Red Phantom" letter

Editor—

Put Marco back in the hell-hole from whence it came—he has a serious psychological disorder—always needs to feel superior. I suggest you refer him to a shrink. Meanwhile, cancel the Count Marco column. Since the Count can write anonymously, so can I—

the Red Phantom
(red with rage)

April 24, 1978
San Francisco, California

The San Francisco Chronicle receives this letter

Dear Editor

This is the Zodiac speaking. I am back with you. Tell herb caen I am here, I have always been here. That city pig toschi is good - but I am smarter and better he will get tired then leave me alone. I am waiting for a good movie about me. who will play me. I am now in control of all things.

Yours truly:

✠ - guess

SFPD - 0

May 2, 1978
San Francisco, California

KHJ-TV receives the "Top Secret Zodiac" letter postmarked May 2, 1978

Dear Channel Nine:

This is the Zodiac speaking. You people in LA are in for a treat. In the next three weeks you are finally gona have something good to report. I have decided to begin Killing again—PLEASE hold the applause! Nothing is going to happen until I do. You people just wont let me have it Any other way. I plan to kill five people in the next three weeks (1) Chief piggy Darrel Gotes (2) Ex Chief piggy Ed Davis (3) Pat Boone—his theocratic crap is a obscenity to the rest of the world! (4) Also Eldrige Cleaver—the niggers gotta get their 20% quota—after all. And Susan Atkins—The Judas of the Manson Family. She's gonna get hers now. Hey-----------you actors----this is your lucky Break. Remember----whoever plays me has their work cut out for them. See you in the Newsw!

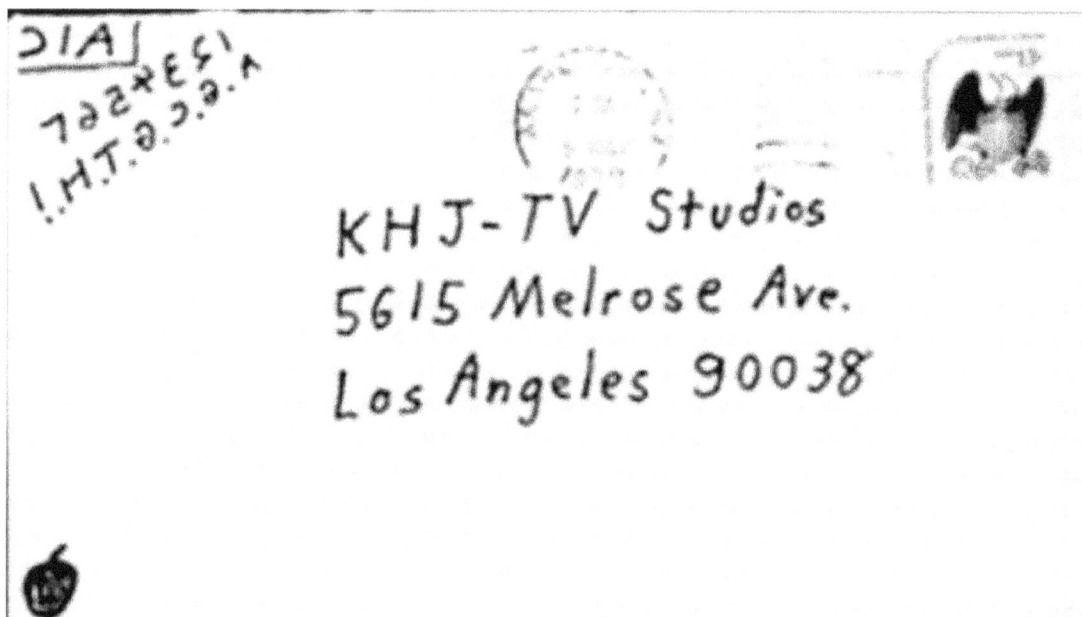

(This envelope contains a clue which is meant to reveal the Zodiac's identity. The clue uses a reference to a Beatles song. The clue has been solved by this author).

THE
FIRST STEPS
AT
BREAKING
THE
CIPHERS

August 8, 1969
Salinas, California

BETTYE and DONALD HARDEN of Salinas, California crack the 408-symbol cipher known as the Z-408 to the level at which the author's letter can be read. While the couple was able to decipher the letter, they stated they could not find the identity of the killer who was soon known as the Zodiac Killer anywhere in the cipher. They concluded—as others would also conclude—that the cipher does not reveal the identity of the Zodiac Killer.

December 12, 2020
San Francisco, California

The San Francisco Chronicle announces that an international codebreaking team comprised of people in the United States, Australia, and Belgium completed the breaking of the Z-340 Cipher. The cipher was first sent to the San Francisco Chronicle in November of 1969. The Federal Bureau of Investigation has confirmed that the team had solved the Z-340.

July 11, 2021
Los Angeles, California

DAVID DANIEL, the Codebreaker who wrote *The Code: The Secret Code Hidden in the English Language*, further breaks the cipher originally known as the Z-408 and the cipher known as the Z-340. He also deciphers the Z-13 Cipher, and solves other clues, discovering once-and-for-all the true identity of the Zodiac Killer.

THE
SUSPECTS

The many lists of Zodiac suspects that can be found on the Internet differ from the list of suspects investigated by the FBI and law enforcement in San Francisco, Vallejo, and Lake Tahoe. New suspects have also been added, but the names of some suspects are pure speculation. A few people have even 'come forward' with the claim that their own father or stepfather was the notorious Zodiac.

There are a number of websites about the Zodiac Killer that list some of the suspects. Some of these websites have gathered an abundance of information regarding the suspects. Information can be found that includes everything from their criminal record to how they became a suspect. These websites have kept the search for the Zodiac Killer going with hopes that someday the killer will be revealed.

The following are some of the men who are now or who have been prime suspects of law enforcement and a few new suspects who have been brought to the attention of the public by their own children or stepchildren. One suspect in this list "confessed" falsely to a friend before he died.

ARTHUR LEIGH ALLEN

ARTHUR LEIGH ALLEN (December 18, 1933 - August 26, 1992), known as LEE ALLEN, was the number one suspect of law enforcement as the Zodiac Killer for many years. In fact, he was interviewed and interrogated for over twenty years. His home was searched numerous times. A number of members of law enforcement have gone to their graves swearing it was him, in spite of the fact that some of the evidence against him is circumstantial. For example, "he wore a Zodiac watch."

He was removed from being an elementary school teacher and arrested for child molestation for which he served time. So, there is evidence of psychopathy. But psychopathy has been found in many of the suspects.

The incriminating evidence includes: (1) MICHAEL MAGEAU, a survivor of the Zodiac, identified Allen in a police photo line-up. (2) Another survivor, BRYAN HARTNELL, identified Allen and his voice as being similar to that of the Zodiac.

On the other hand, eyewitnesses of the Paul Stine murder say he was not the man they saw at the scene. In addition, neither his fingerprints and palm prints nor his handwriting were a match. And Allen did not wear glasses. While he has been officially cleared as a suspect, several die-hards in law enforcement still favor him as the Zodiac.

ROSS MARIO SULLIVAN

ROSS MARIO SULLIVAN (July 28, 1941 - September 29, 1977) has been considered a suspect largely because of (1) his possible link to CHERI JO BATES, a suspected victim, who was murdered in Riverside, California, and because of (2) his strong likeness to the most commonly known police sketch of the Zodiac, as seen here. (3) In addition, he did not report for work after the Bates murder and was missing from work for several days after, and (4) he changed the clothes he usually wore immediately after the murder. (5) He wore military boots that left prints similar to the boot prints found near the crime scene at lake Berryessa. Also, he died in 1977. This is often stated as the possible reason the killings stopped.

There is nothing to indicate sociopathy. Those who knew him did state that they didn't feel comfortable around him and that he wrote "creepy" poems, but this does not suggest sociopathy. He was diagnosed with schizophrenia and bipolar disorder and was hospitalized for these disorders many times.

He has remained on the list of suspects.

RICHARD JOSEPH GAIKOWSKI

RICHARD JOSEPH GAIKOWSKI (March 14, 1936 - April 30, 2004) has been considered a suspect because (1) NANCY STOVER, a police dispatcher who spoke with the Zodiac when he made a call reporting one of his murders, said his voice was the same as or very similar to that of the Zodiac's, (2) during his stay in a mental institution for over nearly three years, there were no letters received from the Zodiac, and (3) in one of the Zodiac's ciphers is the word "GYKE" which was an alleged nickname of GAIKOWSKI. (4) He slightly resembles one of the police sketches. (5) He had a basement in his home and the Zodiac claimed to have a basement.

On the other hand, all so-called evidence is only circumstantial. His likeness isn't strong, having a basement in his home isn't evidence, and neither is the fact that he wore glasses. And he is said to have been 'cleared' by the FBI for fingerprints believed to be from the Zodiac.

In spite of all this, RICHARD JOSEPH GAIKOWSKI has remained on the list of suspects.

LAWRENCE KANE

LAWRENCE KANE (April 29, 1924 - May 10, 2010) went by many surnames. He was born LAWRENCE KLEIN. He changed his name to LAWRENCE KAYE when he was seventeen—stating that it would improve his chances of employment in his line of work. He also used the name LAWRENCE KING. In fact, he was arrested under each of the first three names mentioned, and an arrest report stated that he was committing adultery under the name LAWRENCE KING.

As the result of a car accident in 1962, a psychiatrist stated that due to severe brain damage, he had lost the ability to control self-gratification.

The main reason he became a Zodiac suspect is because (1) he was a suspect in the disappearance of DONNA LASS who was a suspected victim of the Zodiac, (2) He was chosen from a photo line-up by KATHLEEN JOHNS who believed she was abducted by the Zodiac, and (3) he was identified by officer DONALD FOUKE who saw the Zodiac leaving the scene of the murder of PAUL STINE.

While he is not very high on the list of suspects with a resemblance to the more famous police sketch seen here, he is at the top of the list of suspects in resemblance to the first sketch of the Zodiac made by law enforcement.

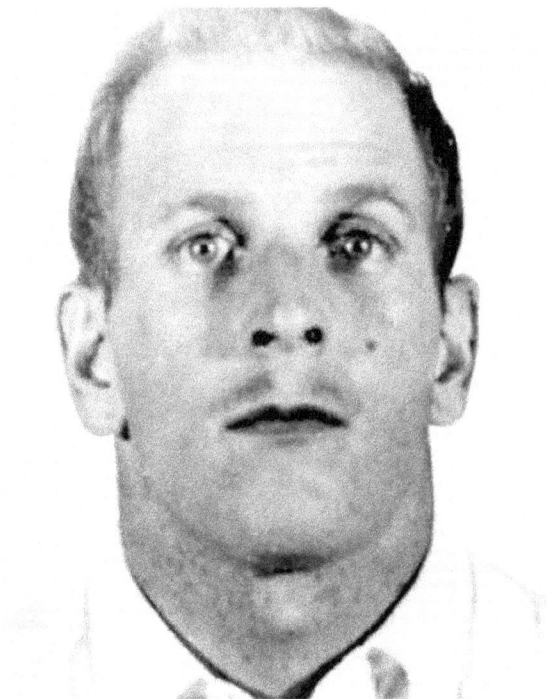

EDWARD WAYNE EDWARDS

EDWARD WAYNE EDWARDS (June 13, 1932 - April 7, 2011) was a convicted American serial killer who was, in addition to his known murders, suspected of other murders—including the murders attributed to the Zodiac Killer. He was on the FBI's Top Ten Most Wanted List in 1961 for robbing gas stations, and he was caught in 1962. After stating he was reformed, he was released and appeared on To Tell the Truth and What's My Line? And he wrote an autobiography on his supposed reform before returning to crime for most of the remainder of his life.

His murders span the late 1970s, the 1980s, and the 1990s. He died of natural causes on April 7, 2011, just four-and-a-half months before he would have been executed by lethal injection.

Because he was a serial killer and he may have lived in the area of San Francisco during some of the periods of time of the Zodiac killings, he is on the list of suspects.

GARY FRANCIS POSTE

GARY FRANCIS POSTE (November 8, 1937 - August 31, 2018) was named as a suspect in a press release as the Zodiac Killer by a team of researchers and experts and military investigators calling themselves the Case Breakers.

The major reason for their belief in this suspect is (1) the scars on the forehead in the most well-known police sketch of the Zodiac appeared to match the scars on the forehead of GARY FRANCIS POSTE. This is in addition to (2) the scary likeness between the two. There was a lot of interest in the media regarding their press release.

But soon after all the buzz, the Federal Bureau of Investigation stated that the Zodiac Killer case was still open. In other words, the FBI found no interest in GARY FRANCIS POSTE. The team also believes that GARY FRANCIS POSTE killed a woman in Riverside named CHERYL JO BATES, but this belief is also brushed off—this one by the police in Riverside.

EARL VAN BEST JR

EARL VAN BEST JR (July 14, 1934 - May 20, 1984) became a suspect through his son, GARY STEWART, who he had abandoned.

STEWART believed his father was the Zodiac Killer and co-authored a book about his journey to discover his father's 'true' identity. He believed this to be true because (1) his father lived in San Francisco at the time of the murders and (2) had a such a strong resemblance to one of the Zodiac sketches, STEWART claims his father was, in fact, the Zodiac Killer.

There is nothing one could call evidence — incriminating or circumstantial — that suggested that EARL VAN BEST JR was ever involved in anything of this nature. He is included here because he is on most lists of suspects and because of his resemblance to the most commonly shown police sketch.

He is the first of three suspects who became suspects on the suspicions of their son or stepson.

GEORGE HILL HODEL JR

GEORGE HILL HODEL JR (October 10, 1907 - May 16, 1999) became a suspect through his son, STEVE HODEL, a retired police detective. STEVE wrote a book about his suspicions and investigations in his book *THE BLACK DAHLIA AVENGER*. In the book, his father, GEORGE HODEL was a major suspect in the murder of ELIZABETH SHORT, better known as the BLACK DAHLIA. According to the book, his father was in fact, the BLACK DAHLIA KILLER. Many members of law enforcement believed that the killer was, indeed, GEORGE HILL HODEL JR.

While the evidence was already strong that his father was the BLACK DAHLIA KILLER, and was suspected of being a serial killer, STEVE HODEL took his imagination to a new level—claiming his father was the ZODIAC.

While GEORGE HILL HODEL JR could very likely have been the BLACK DAHLIA KILLER, there is absolutely no evidence that he was the ZODIAC. No descriptions given by witnesses suggested a man of the age of 61 or 62, and he looked nothing like any police sketch.

JOHN WALKER "JACK" TARRANCE

JOHN WALKER TARRANCE JR (February 24, 1928 - August 31, 2005) became a suspect through his supposed stepson, Dennis Kaufman.

The evidence was presented to the police by the stepson and was as follows: (1) handwriting samples he collected of his father, (2) a knife with dried blood that he claimed had belonged to his father, and (3) a homemade hood he believed resembled the one the Zodiac Killer had worn during his murder at Lake Berryessa.

There is actually no real evidence, circumstantial, incriminating, or otherwise to support his stepson's belief or accusation that JACK TARRANCE was the ZODIAC.

This is the third suspect who was put on the list by a son or stepson. Who would want their father to be a serial killer? A number of people have made claims that their parents or ex-partners, or siblings are or were serial killers.

JOE DON DICKEY

JOE DON DICKEY (March 13, 1926 - September 8, 2008) used his born name and his alias RICHARD REED MARSHALL throughout his life. He also gave several alternative birthdates.

During the time of most of the Zodiac Killer's letters and ciphers and known murders, DICKEY was working at a silent movie theatre in San Francisco. He didn't become a suspect until 1976 when (1) he said a few suspicious things over his ham radio.

His interviews with police produced nothing and the evidence against him was entirely circumstantial. He was, however, investigated for a very long time and remained a good suspect for some time.

He is considered by some to remain a suspect in spite of the Napa Sheriff's conclusion that he was cleared of being the Zodiac.

LOUIS JOSEPH MYERS

LOUIS JOSEPH MYERS (June 10, 1951 - May 6, 2002) was quite young at the time of the murders and only seventeen years old at the time of the first.

It is alleged by his best friend that (1) he confessed to having been the Zodiac Killer with a promise from his friend not to go to the police until he was dead, (2) saying a break-up and heartbreak led him to kill couples. (3) He attended the same high schools of two of the victims, (4) and worked at the same restaurant as another victim.

A number of people have confessed to the Zodiac killings. In fact, whenever there is a serial killer, multiple people confess. It is more common than not for this to happen.

There is only circumstantial evidence. Nonetheless, LOUIS JOSEPH MYERS remains on the list of suspects.

WILLIAM JOSEPH GRANT

WILLIAM JOSEPH GRANT (March 6, 1920 - February 2, 2012) used at least three other names. He became known to the police in April 1970 when he played games in traffic with a highway patrolman who finally saw him and was shocked by the hatred in his face.

The evidence of him being the Zodiac includes the following: (1) he was not at work during the killings and no killings occurred when he was at work, (2) he was ambidextrous and the Zodiac was believed to be ambidextrous, (3) he was a regular customer at a restaurant where one of the suspected victims was a waitress.

He was considered a good suspect for many years, and he remains on the list of possible suspects for being the Zodiac Killer.

FINDING

THE

ZODIAC

In July 2021, I was reading about the serial killer who is known as the Zodiac Killer. I read about the murders and the victims and about many of the suspects. I kept reading because I was curious about why he had never been caught or identified. I thought about how the victims and their families and their other loved ones need closure. Journalists need to know. The public needs to know. Law enforcement needs to close the case.

After reading a little more about the case, I read about the cipher known as the Z-408 that the Zodiac had sent to several newspapers.

He sent his first known ciphers and his first known letters to three newspapers—the Vallejo Times Herald, the San Francisco Examiner, and the San Francisco Chronicle on July 31, 1969. They were published by the respective newspapers. Within a short time, a married couple, Bettye and Donald Harden, had cracked the three ciphers which together contained a letter from the Zodiac.

In his letter sent to the San Francisco Chronicle, the Zodiac stated, "In this cipher is my identity." Law Enforcement stated that the cipher did not reveal his identity but I took the man for his word. I knew that it was there and I knew that I would find it.

When he wrote "In this cipher is my identity," that was an invitation to anyone who was really listening. And I accepted it. I didn't think, "I am going to try to find his identity." I merely thought to myself, "I will find his identity."

I invite you to take this journey with me as we find this notorious serial killer together.

One of the suspects you have just read about was, in fact, the long-sought Zodiac Killer.

The Zodiac sent this cipher to the Vallejo Times Herald. This is the Ciphertext. Ciphertext is an encrypted text. It can consist of letters, characters, numbers, and/or symbols. It is the result of someone encrypting a Plaintext—often for the sake of concealing its message. Once it is Ciphertext, someone must find the key to the cipher and use the key to "crack" or decipher or decrypt it in order to find the Plaintext which is the original message.

The letters from the Plaintext are printed here just above the Ciphertext. Plaintext is an unencrypted text—that is—it is the original message before it has been encrypted. It is also the decrypted text—the text that is found after a cipher has been "cracked" or deciphered—which is to say that it is the same as the original text that existed before it was encrypted. Bettye and Donald Harden deciphered the Ciphertext which resulted in this readable Plaintext.

I was prepared to examine the cipher, but I didn't have to.

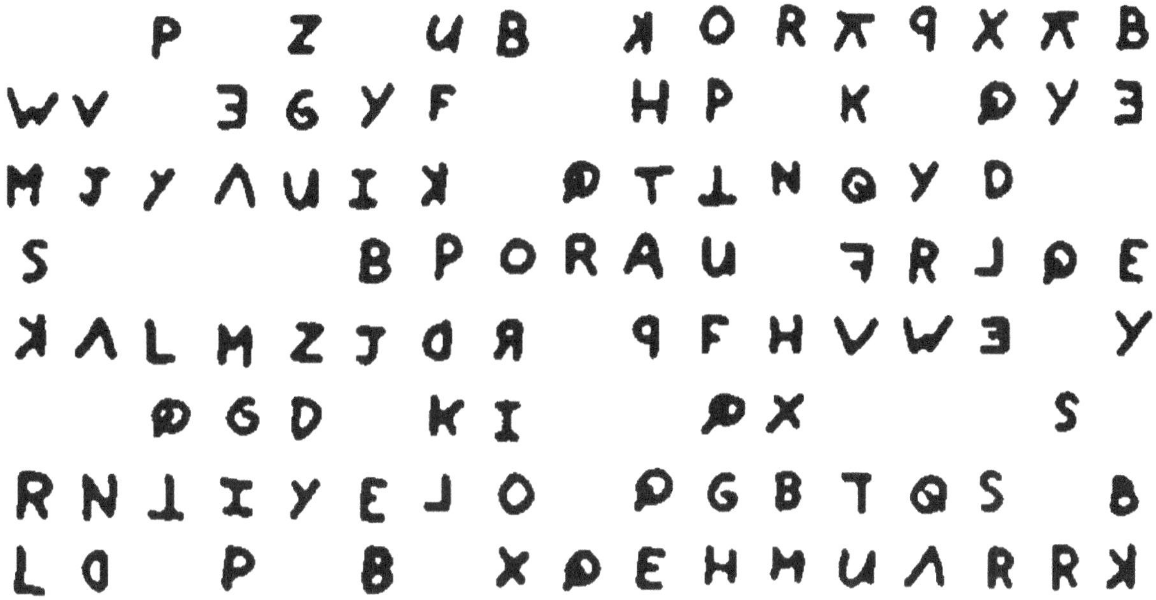

P　Z　U B　Ʌ O R Ɱ ꟼ X Ɱ B

ꟽ Ʌ　Ǝ G Y F　　H P　K　Ꝺ Y Ǝ

M Ꞁ Y Ʌ U I Ʞ　Ꝺ T ⊥ ᴎ Ǫ Y D

S　　　　B P O R A U　ꟻ R Ꞁ Ꝺ Ǝ

Ʞ Ʌ L M Z Ꞁ ᴑ Я　ꟼ F H V ʍ Ǝ　　Y

　Ꝺ G D　K I　　Ꝺ X　　　　S

R N ⊥ I Y Ǝ O　Ꝺ G B T Ǫ S　ᕐ

L ᴑ　P　B　X Ꝺ Ǝ H ᴎ U Ʌ R R Ʞ

In the first instant I noticed that the Ciphertext was filled with letters from the alphabet in various positions. Many were in their regular position; some were reversed (backwards); some were inverted (upside down); one was rotated (sideways).

א   א   א

K

א

א

K

א

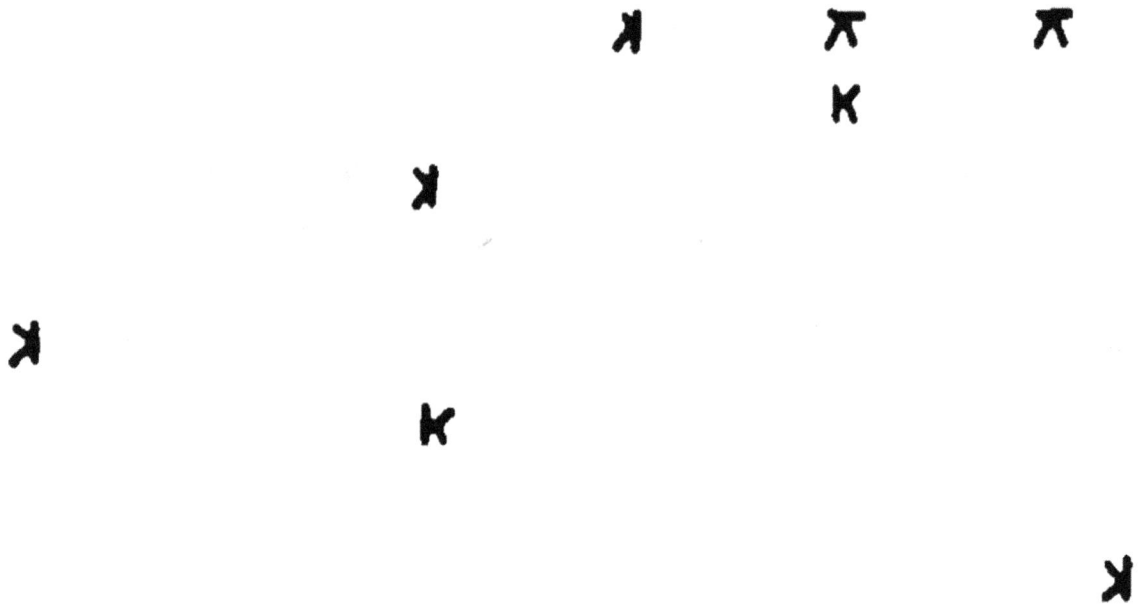

And an instant later, I noticed that four 'K's were in the upper right area, and four more 'K's were spread across the Ciphertext. All of the other letters were in one or two positions but the letter K was the only letter in three—regular position, reversed, and rotated.

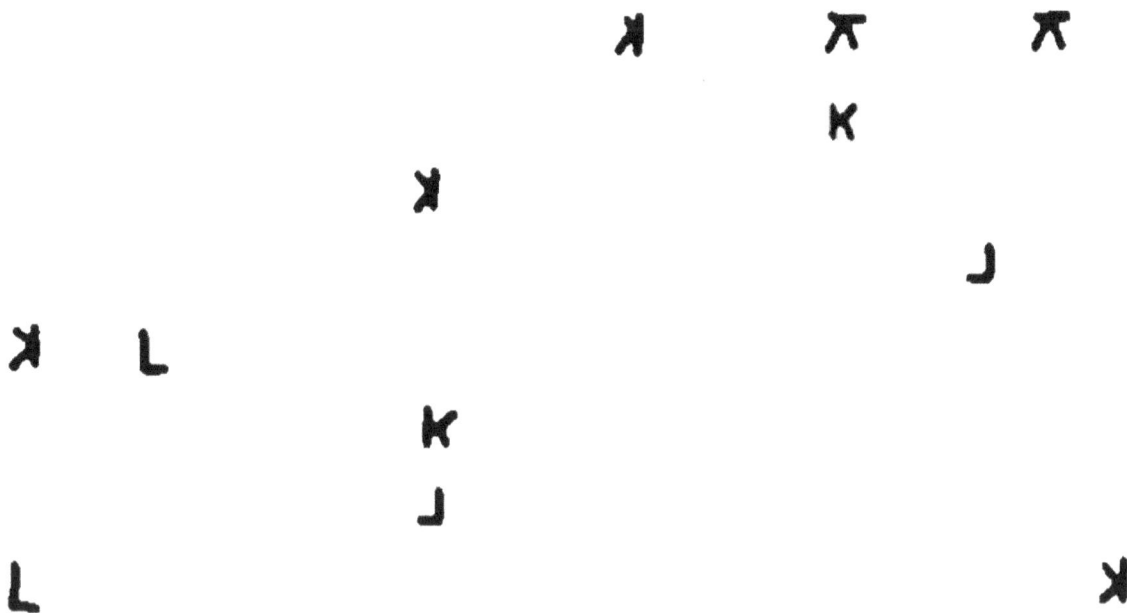

One of the suspects had an initial K. As his other initial is L, I looked and noticed that there were also some 'L's. In the lower left corner, there was an L in its regular position facing its right and in the lower right corner there was a K facing its left. In fact, it was facing the L.

These two letters—LK—are the initials of a leading suspect—LARRY KLEIN/LARRY KANE/LARRY KAYE/LARRY KING. And his initials are in the left and right lower corners facing each other. This is in addition to the manipulation of the Ks in the cipher.

For me, the identity of the Zodiac was solved in three to seven seconds.

But I continued. And I knew there would be 'K's and 'L's in the Plaintext in the upper left area to make up for the fact that there were no 'K's or 'L's in the Ciphertext in the upper left area.

I L I K E K I L L I N G P E O P L
E B E C A U S E I T I S S O M U C
H F U N I T I S M O R E F U N T H
A N K I L L I N G W I L D G A M E
I N T H E F O R R E S T B E C A U
S E M A N I S T H E M O S T D A N
G E R O U E A N A M A L O F A L L
T O K I L L S O M E T H I N G G I

So, I looked at the Ciphertext paired together with the Plaintext. I had no doubt at all that they would be there.

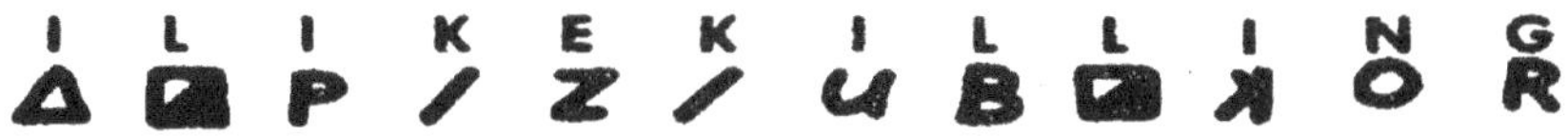

I L I K E K I L L I N G
△ ▣ P ╱ Z ╱ ⊔ B ▣ ⅄ Ø R

K I L L I N G
╱ △ ■ B P O R

K I L L
╱ P ▰ B

And they were. There were a number of words containing 'K's and 'L's and two of them had other letters that were in his names.

In the Plaintext where I saw "I LIKE KILLING", "KILLING", and "KILL" there were 4 'K's, 7 'L's, 7 'I's, 2 'G's, and 2 'N's in these three messages. These are the letters in KLEIN, KANE, KAYE, and KING.

I LIKE KILLING

KILLING

KILL

So, I added these words....

To these 'K's and 'L's....

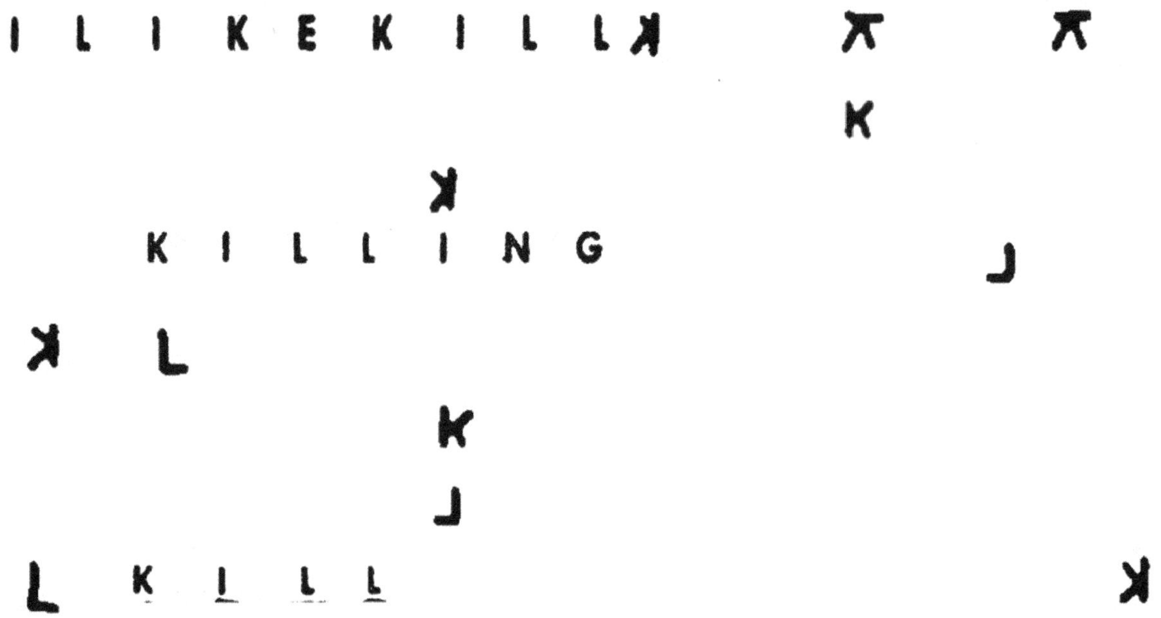

I L I K E K I L L K ⊼ ⊼

K

K

K I L L I N G J

K L

K

J

L K I L L K

And I got this.

The 'K's and 'L's were now spread to the left side of the cipher, including in the upper left area.

Let us examine this first cipher more closely. We can see it was meant to be read first as it contained the beginning of a letter. I noticed several curiosities right away. As I said, the majority of the characters in the cipher are letters of the alphabet in various positions. That is, some of the letters are in their regular position, some are reversed (backwards), some are inverted (upside down), and one is rotated (you might say it is on its side). All the letters are in only one or two positions—except for one.

The one letter that is in three positions is the letter K. It can be seen in its regular position K, reversed Ʞ, and rotated ⅄, with eight appearances of the letter K.

In this way, the letter K is splattered all over the cipher.

Obviously, this was on purpose—a manipulation. The only real outcome is that the letter K is scattered all over the cipher.

K   Ʞ   ⅄

REGULAR POSITION   REVERSED   ROTATED

Before we go on, it is very important for me to acknowledge and to actually address the fact that a number of letters in various positions have a meaning in other contexts—for example, in the world of astrology. It is obvious to me that the Zodiac assumed many people viewing his ciphers would believe this was the case. The rotated K, the reversed C, and the inverted V are just a few examples of astrological symbols being identical to letters of the alphabet in their normal position or in another position. This does nothing to invalidate the Zodiac's intent of using these symbols as letters of the alphabet in the cipher.

Upon further examination of the cipher, it appeared to me that the Zodiac was manipulating the Ciphertext in order to increase the distribution of the letter K in the cipher. There could only be one reason why he would concern himself with what is in the Ciphertext.

Ultimately, the Zodiac intended for the Ciphertext to be included in a Final Text of the cipher. And so, I thought that there must be an extra-secret Final Text which is where the Zodiac would reveal his identity.

In the Plaintext, I found "I LIKE KILLING." Here we also see the letter K twice in just those three words, the letter L three times, the letter I three times and we see an E, an N, and a G. These are all letters of the Zodiac's four surnames—KLEIN/KANE/KAYE/KING.

After analyzing the Plaintext and the Ciphertext, I realized that the two texts were intended to be blended so that a Final Text would emerge. And, so, it came to me that the Plaintext was so much more than just a letter that said, "I LIKE KILLING." Rather, the Plaintext was painstakingly constructed to complement the letters in the Ciphertext in order to reveal the Zodiac's identity all over the Final Text.

I looked for a presentation of the two texts together—the Ciphertext and the Plaintext.

I quickly found a presentation of the two texts together and I could clearly see that the spread of the letters was there for a purpose. It became obvious that the appearance of the Zodiac's surnames—KLEIN/KANE/KAYE/KING—often with his first initial L, could be found throughout the Final Text. I identified the most probable focus of the Zodiac. If you go across the Blended Text creating 4-by-4 blocks, you find numerous blocks with one or more of his names—some have three or four of his names in a block. I realized the Zodiac deliberately constructed the cipher using 4-by-4 blocks for the purpose of identifying himself.

The Blended Text is the intentional Final Text of the three ciphers known as the Z-408 that he sent on July 31, 1969. I call the first cipher of the Z-408 the Z-136-A or the "Times Herald Cipher."

THE NAMES

OF THE

ZODIAC KILLER

REVEALED MULTIPLE TIMES

IN THE 'FINAL TEXT' OF

THE CIPHER

HE SENT TO THE

VALLEJO TIMES HERALD

JULY 31, 1969

"THE TIMES HERALD CIPHER"

Z-136-A

BLENDED TEXT

This is the cipher that was sent to the Vallejo Times Herald newspaper. Here we see the Ciphertext paired together with the Plaintext. This is the cipher that contains multiple reveals of the Zodiac Killer's name, signed and initialed by the Zodiac, himself.

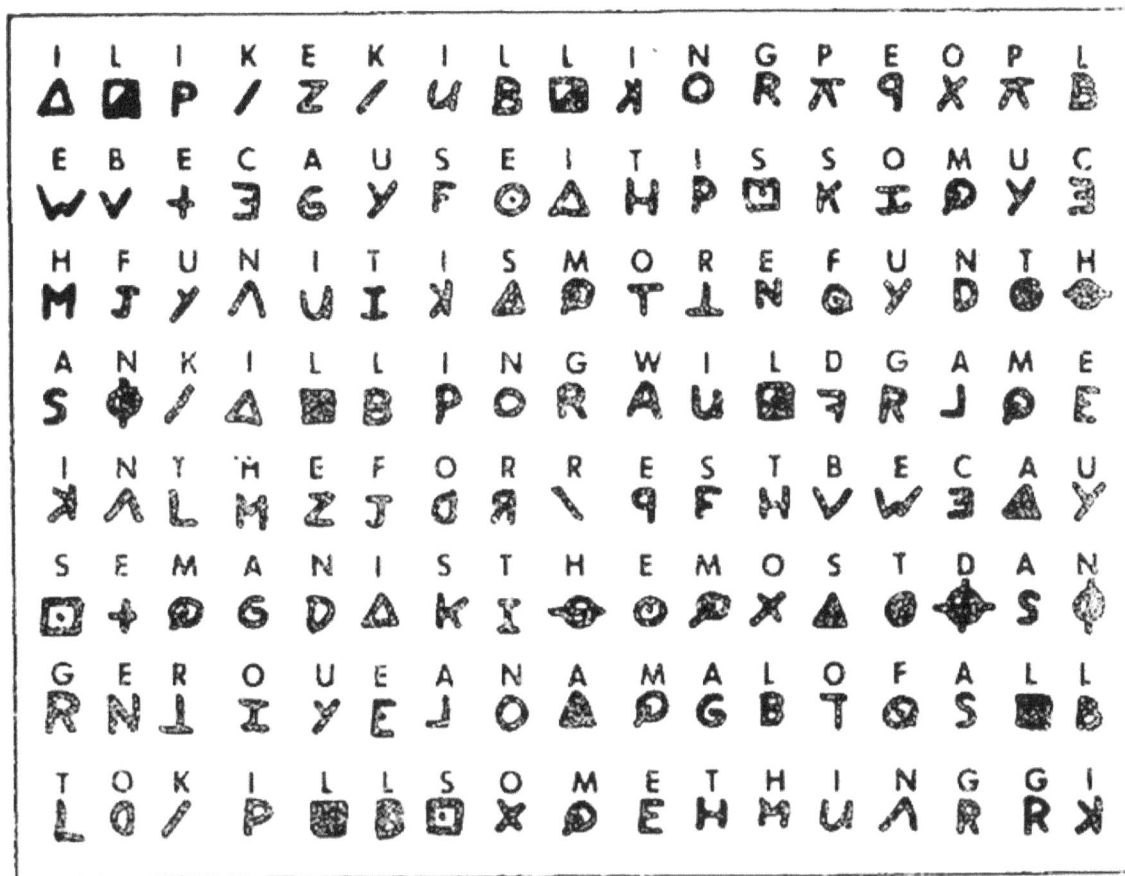

The majority of the characters in the cipher are letters. Some of them are in their regular position, some are backwards, upside down or sideways. Only one letter in the cipher is in three positions and that is the letter K. We find it in its regular position, in reverse and rotated. In fact, the letter K is all over the page. This made me curious as to why he was doing this, especially as one of the suspects has a last name beginning with the letter K. I examined the cipher carefully. One of the major suspects was born LAWRENCE "LARRY" KLEIN, but he had used the names LARRY KANE, LARRY KAYE, and LARRY KING.

I eventually chose to include a study of all letters in the Plaintext and Ciphertext in 4-by-4 blocks. That is, I would use the characters from the Ciphertext that were actual letters—no matter if they were in their regular position, in reverse, inverted or rotated—and blend them with the letters in the Plaintext. For example, **G** is a substitution for **R**.

I decided to examine the Final Text from left to right in 4-by-4 blocks. The first 4-by-4 block is in the upper left corner. I call it A-Block—1. It contains 4 characters across and 4 characters down.

To clarify what I mean, the upper left 4-by-4 block begins with a **Δ** with a small **I** just above it, and it contains the first four characters at the top from left to right. The 4th is a **/** with a **K** right above it. The bottom right corner of this block is also a **Δ**.

In this block, we see the Plaintext horizontally reads ILIK across and vertically IEHA. The I in the upper left corner is just above a **Δ** which is the first character in the Ciphertext. The fourth letter over is a K which is just above a **/**. The letters in the Plaintext in the first 4-by-4 block (4 letters across and 4 letters down) reads ILIKEBECHFUNANKI. While non-alphabetical symbols are also in the first 4-by-4 block, there are many letters in the Ciphertext. These are P in the first row, WV and a reversed E in the second row, MJY in the third row, and only an S in the bottom row of this block.

Never mind that some letters are in reverse, inverted, or rotated. The Zodiac used this as a trick in order to splatter his name all over the page.

The blocks are identified from where they are lined up horizontally and vertically. The top line in each block is one identifier. If it is the first line across, it is A, the second line across is B, and so on. So, this identifies it as A-Block or B-Block and so on all the way to E-Block. The second identifier is the column it is in. The first column from the left is 1, the second is 2, and so on, with the last block which is 14.

Thus, the first block in the cipher is A-BLOCK—1. The final block is E-BLOCK—14.

For each character in the Ciphertext, there is a letter from the Plaintext right above it. I call each of these a set. For example, the first character in the Ciphertext is a **Δ** and right above it is the letter I. The **Δ** and the letter I are the first set in the cipher. You will notice quite often that the letters that spell one of the Zodiac's names each come from a different set.

In addition to the reveal of his four names multiple times in the following presentations, we also find obvious messages in the ciphers such as "I AM THE ZODIAC" and "MY NAME IS." There also appear to be other messages. I only include a few examples of other possible messages to show that the Zodiac was not only using the ciphers to reveal his names but to sneak in other taunts as well. The major objective of these presentations is to demonstrate how the Zodiac manipulated the Ciphertext and Plaintext in order to construct a Final Text that reveals his identity multiple times.

A-BLOCK—1 (above)
1. KLEIN
2. L KAYE
3. L KANE

A-BLOCK—2 (below)
1. L KLEIN
2. L KAYE
3. L KANE
4. L KING

A-BLOCK—3 (above)
  1. L KLEIN
  2. L KAYE
  3. L KANE
  4. L KING

A-BLOCK—4 (below)
  1. L KLEIN
  2. L KAYE
  3. L KANE
  4. L KING

A-BLOCK—5 (above)
1. L KLEIN
2. L KAYE
3. L KANE
4. L KING

A-BLOCK—6 (below)
1. L KLEIN
2. L KING

I L I K E K I L L I N G P E O P L
E B E C A U S E I T I S S O M U C
H F U N I T I S M O R E F U N T H
A N K I L L I N G W I L D G A M E
I N T H E F O R R E S T B E C A U
S E M A N I S T H E M O S T D A N
G E R O U E A N A M A L O F A L L
T O K I L L S O M E T H I N G G I

A-BLOCK—7 (above)
1. L KLEIN
2. L KANE
3. L KING

A-BLOCK—8 (below)
1. L KLEIN
2. L KANE
3. L KING

I L I K E K I L L I N O G P E O P L
E B E C A U S F E I T I P S O M U C
H F U N I T I X S M O R E N U N T H
A N K I L L I P N G W I U L D G A M E
I N T H E F O R R E S T H V W B E C A U
S E M A N I S T H E M O S T D A N
G E R O U E A N A M A L O F A L L
T O K I L L S O M E T H I N G G I

I L I K E K I L L I N G P E O P L E
E B E C A U S E I T I S S O M U C H
H F U N I T I S M O R E F U N T H
A N K I L L I N G W I L D G A M E
I N T H E F O R R E S T B E C A U
S E M A N I S T H E M O S T D A N
G E R O U E A N A M A L O F A L L
T O K I L L S O M E T H I N G G I

A-BLOCK—9 (above)
1. L KLEIN
2. L KANE
3. L KING

A-BLOCK—10 (below)
1. KLEIN
2. L KANE
3. L KING

I L I K E K I L L I N G P E O P L E
E B E C A U S E I T I S S O M U C H
H F U N I T I S M O R E F U N T H
A N K I L L I N G W I L D G A M E
I N T H E F O R R E S T B E C A U
S E M A N I S T H E M O S T D A N
G E R O U E A N A M A L O F A L L
T O K I L L S O M E T H I N G G I

A-BLOCK—11 (above)

I L I K E K I L L I N G P E O P L
E B E C A U S E I T I S S O M U C
H F U N I T I S M O R E F U N T H
A N K I L L I N G W I L D G A M E
I N T H E F O R R E S T B E C A U
S E M A N I S T H E M O S T D A N
G E R O U E A N A M A L O F A L L
T O K I L L S O M E T H I N G G I

A-BLOCK—11 (above)
1. KLEIN
2. L KING

A-BLOCK—12 (below)
1. LARRY K
2. L KANE
3. L KAYE

I L I K E K I L L I N G P E O P L
E B E C A U S E I T I S S O M U C
H F U N I T I S M O R E F U N T H
A N K I L L I N G W I L D G A M E
I N T H E F O R R E S T B E C A U
S E M A N I S T H E M O S T D A N
G E R O U E A N A M A L O F A L L
T O K I L L S O M E T H I N G G I

Note: The character in the Ciphertext that substitutes for an O is not an I. There is a strong resemblance but the bottom of the character is not a straight line. Also, a character cannot stand for more than one letter. The I in this cipher substitutes for a T.

97

I LIKE KILLING PEOPLE

```
I L I K E K I L L I N G   N O   G R   P E O P L   B
E B E C A U S E I T I S   S O   M U   C E
H F U N I T I S M O R E   N   F U N T   H
A N K I L L I N G W I L D   G A M E   E
I N T H E F O R R E S T   B E C A U   Y
S E M A N I S T H E M O S T D A N
G E R O U E A N A M A L O F A L L
T O K I L L S O M E T H I N G G I K
```

A-BLOCK—13 (above)
  1. L KANE
  2. L KAYE

A-BLOCK—14 (below)
  1. L KANE
  2. L KAYE
  3. "MY NAME…"

```
I L I K E K I L L I N G   N O   G R   P E O P L   B
E B E C A U S E I T I S   S O   M U   C E
H F U N I T I S M O R E   N   F U N T   H
A N K I L L I N G W I L D   G A M E   E
I N T H E F O R R E S T   B E C A U   Y
S E M A N I S T H E M O S T D A N
G E R O U E A N A M A L O F A L L
T O K I L L S O M E T H I N G G I K
```

I L I K E K I L L I N G P E O P L

E B E C A U S E I T I S S O M U C

H F U N I T I S M O R E F U N T H

A N K I L L I N G W I L D G A M E

I N T H E F O R R E S T B E C A U

S E M A N I S T H E M O S T D A N

G E R O U E A N A M A L O F A L L

T O K I L L S O M E T H I N G G I K

B-BLOCK—1 (above)
1. KLEIN
2. L KAYE
3. L KANE

B-BLOCK—2
1. L KLEIN
2. L KAYE
3. L KANE
4. L KING

I L I K E K I L L I N G P E O P L

E B E C A U S E I T I S S O M U C

H F U N I T I S M O R E F U N T H

A N K I L L I N G W I L D G A M E

I N T H E F O R R E S T B E C A U

S E M A N I S T H E M O S T D A N

G E R O U E A N A M A L O F A L L

T O K I L L S O M E T H I N G G I K

I L I K E K I L L I N G P E O P L
E B E C A U S E I T I S S O M U C E
H F U N I T I S M O R E F U N T H
A N K I L L I N G W I L D G A M E E
I N T H E F O R R E S T B E C A U
S E M A N I S T H E M O S T D A N
G E R O U E A N A M A L O F A L L
T O K I L L S O M E T H I N G G I K

B-BLOCK—3 (above)
1. "I AM L KLEIN"
2. L KAYE
3. L KANE
4. I AM L KING
5. "I AM THE…"

B-BLOCK—4 (below)
1. L KLEIN
2. L KAYE
3. L KANE
4. L KING
5. "I'M THE ZODIAC"

I L I K E K I L L I N G P E O P L
E B E C A U S E I T I S S O M U C E
H F U N I T I S M O R E F U N T H
A N K I L L I N G W I L D G A M E E
I N T H E F O R R E S T B E C A U
S E M A N I S T H E M O S T D A N
G E R O U E A N A M A L O F A L L
T O K I L L S O M E T H I N G G I K

100

I L I K E K I L L I N G P E O P L E
E B E C A U S E I T I S S O M U C E
H F U N I T I S M O R E F U N T H
A N K I L L I N G W I L D G A M E
I N T H E F O R R E S T B E C A U
S E M A N I S T H E M O S T D A N
G E R O U E A N A M A L O F A L L
T O K I L L S O M E T H I N G G I K

B-BLOCK—5 (above)
1. LARRY KLEIN
2. LARRY KING
3. L KANE
4. L KAYE

B-BLOCK—6 (below)
1. KLEIN
2. L KING

I L I K E K I L L I N G P E O P L E
E B E C A U S E I T I S S O M U C E
H F U N I T I S M O R E F U N T H
A N K I L L I N G W I L D G A M E
I N T H E F O R R E S T B E C A U
S E M A N I S T H E M O S T D A N
G E R O U E A N A M A L O F A L L
T O K I L L S O M E T H I N G G I K

101

B-BLOCK—7 (above)
1. KANE
2. KING

B-BLOCK—8 (below)
1. "I AM THE ONE"

102

I L I K E K I L L I N G P E O P L
E B E C A U S E I T I S S O M U C
H F U N I T I S M O R E F U N T H
A N K I L L I N G W I L D G A M E
I N T H E F O R R E S T B E C A U
S E M A N I S T H E M O S T D A N
G E R O U E A N A M A L O F A L L
T O K I L L S O M E T H I N G G I K

B-BLOCK—9 (above)
1. "I AM THE ONE"
2. "I AM HIM"

B-BLOCK—10 (below)
1. KLEIN
2. L KANE

I L I K E K I L L I N G P E O P L
E B E C A U S E I T I S S O M U C
H F U N I T I S M O R E F U N T H
A N K I L L I N G W I L D G A M E
I N T H E F O R R E S T B E C A U
S E M A N I S T H E M O S T D A N
G E R O U E A N A M A L O F A L L
T O K I L L S O M E T H I N G G I K

I L I K E K I L L I N G P E O P L
E B E C A U S E I T I S S O M U C
H F U N I T I S M O R E F U N T H
A N K I L L I N G W I L D G A M E
I N T H E F O R R E S T B E C A U
S E M A N I S T H E M O S T D A N
G E R O U E A N A M A L O F A L L
T O K I L L S O M E T H I N G

B-BLOCK—11 (above)
1. KLEIN
2. L KING

B-BLOCK—12 (below)
1. L KANE
2. L KAYE

I L I K E K I L L I N G P E O P L
E B E C A U S E I T I S S O M U C
H F U N I T I S M O R E F U N T H
A N K I L L I N G W I L D G A M E
I N T H E F O R R E S T B E C A U
S E M A N I S T H E M O S T D A N
G E R O U E A N A M A L O F A L L
T O K I L L S O M E T H I N G

B-BLOCK—13 (above)
1. L KANE
2. L KAYE
3. "MY NAME"

B-BLOCK—14 (below)
1. "MY NAME"

105

C-BLOCK—1 (above)
1. KLEIN
2. L KAYE
3. L KANE
4. L KING

C-BLOCK—2 (below)
1. L KLEIN
2. L KAYE
3. L KANE
4. L KING

C-BLOCK—3 (above)
1. L KLEIN
2. L KANE
3. L KAYE
4. L KING

C-BLOCK—4 (below)
1. L KLEIN
2. L KANE
3. L KING

C-BLOCK—5 (above)
   1. L KLEIN

C-BLOCK—6 (below)
   1. L KING

I L I K E K I L L I N G P E O P L
E B E C A U S E I T I S S O M U C
H F U N I T I S M O R E F U N T H
A N K I L L I N G W I L D G A M E
I N T H E F O R R E S T B E C A U
S E M A N I S T H E M O S T D A N
G E R O U E A N A M A L O F A L L
T O K I L L S O M E T H I N G G I

C-BLOCK—7 (above)
1. KANE
2. KING

I L I K E K I L L I N G P E O P L
E B E C A U S E I T I S S O M U C
H F U N I T I S M O R E F U N T H
A N K I L L I N G W I L D G A M E
I N T H E F O R R E S T B E C A U
S E M A N I S T H E M O S T D A N
G E R O U E A N A M A L O F A L L
T O K I L L S O M E T H I N G G I

D-BLOCK—1 (above)

1. KLEIN
2. L KANE
3. L KING

D-BLOCK—2 (below)

1. L KLEIN
2. L KAYE
3. L KANE
4. L KING

I L I K E K I L L I N G P E O P L
E B E C A U S E I T I S S O M U C
H F U N I T I S M O R E F U N T H
A N K I L L I N G W I L D G A M E
I N T H E F O R R E S T B E C A U
S E M A N I S T H E M O S T D A N
G E R O U E A N A M A L O F A L L
T O K I L L S O M E T H I N G G I

D-BLOCK—3 (above)
1. L KLEIN
2. L KAYE
3. L KANE
4. L KING

D-BLOCK—4 (below)
1. L KLEIN
2. L KAYE
3. L KANE
4. L KING

I L I K E K I L L I N G P E O P L
E B E C A U S E I T I S S O M U C
H F U N I T I S M O R E F U N T H
A N K I L L I N G W I L D G A M E
I N T H E F O R R E S T B E C A U
S E M A N I S T H E M O S T D A N
G E R O U E A N A M A L O F A L L
T O K I L L S O M E T H I N G G I

D-BLOCK—5 (above)
1. L KLEIN
2. L KAYE
3. L KANE

D-BLOCK—6 (below)
1. L KLEIN
2. L KANE
3. L KING

I L I K E K I L L I N G P E O P L
E B E C A U S E I T I S S O M U C
H F U N I T I S M O R E F U N T H
A N K I L L I N G W I L D G A M E
I N T H E F O R R E S T B E C A U
S E M A N I S T H E M O S T D A N
G E R O U E A N A M A L O F A L L
T O K I L L S O M E T H I N G G I

112

I L I K E K I L L I N G P E O P L
E B E C A U S E I T I S S O M U C
H F U N I T I S M O R E F U N T H
A N K I L L I N G W I L D G A M E
I N T H E F O R R E S T B E C A U
S E M A N I S T H E M O S T D A N
G E R O U E A N A M A L O F A L L
T O K I L L S O M E T H I N G G I

D-BLOCK—7 (above)
  1. KLEIN
  2. L KANE
  3. L KING

I L I K E K I L L I N G P E O P L
E B E C A U S E I T I S S O M U C E
H F U N I T I S M O R E F U N T H
A N K I L L I N G W I L D G A M E E
I N T H E F O R R E S T B E C A U
S E M A N I S T H E M O S T D A N
G E R O U E A N A M A L O F A L L
T O K I L L S O M E T H I N G G I K

E-BLOCK—1 (above)
1. L KLEIN
2. L KANE
3. L KING

E-BLOCK—2 (below)
1. L KLEIN
2. L KAYE
3. L KANE
4. L KING

I L I K E K I L L I N G P E O P L
E B E C A U S E I T I S S O M U C E
H F U N I T I S M O R E F U N T H
A N K I L L I N G W I L D G A M E E
I N T H E F O R R E S T B E C A U
S E M A N I S T H E M O S T D A N
G E R O U E A N A M A L O F A L L
T O K I L L S O M E T H I N G G I K

114

I L I K E K   L   I   N G P E O P L
E B E C A U S E I T I S   S O M U C
H F U N I T I S   M O R E F U N T H
A N K I L L I N G W I L D G A M E E
I N T H E F O R R E S T B E C A U
S E M A N I S T H E M O S T D A N
G E R O U E A N A M A L O F A L L
T O K I L L S O M E T H I N G G I K

E-BLOCK—3 (above)
1. L KLEIN
2. L KAYE
3. L KANE
4. L KING

E-BLOCK—4 (below)
1. L KLEIN
2. L KAYE
3. L KANE
4. L KING

I L I K E K   L   I   N G P E O P L
E B E C A U S E I T I S   S O M U C
H F U N I T I S   M O R E F U N T H
A N K I L L I N G W I L D G A M E E
I N T H E F O R R E S T B E C A U
S E M A N I S T H E M O S T D A N
G E R O U E A N A M A L O F A L L
T O K I L L S O M E T H I N G G I K

115

I L I K E K I L L I N G P E O P L
E B E C A U S E I T I S S O M U C
H F U N I T I S M O R E F U N T H
A N K I L L I N G W I L D G A M E E
I N T H E F O R R E S T B E C A U
S E M A N I S T H E M O S T D A N
G E R O U E A N A M A L O F A L L
T O K I L L S O M E T H I N G G I R

E-BLOCK—5 (above)
1. L KLEIN
2. L KAYE
3. L KANE

E-BLOCK—6 (below)
1. L KLEIN
2. L KANE

I L I K E K I L L I N G P E O P L
E B E C A U S E I T I S S O M U C
H F U N I T I S M O R E F U N T H
A N K I L L I N G W I L D G A M E E
I N T H E F O R R R E S T B E C A U
S E M A N I S T H E M O S T D A N
G E R O U E A N A M A L O F A L L
T O K I L L S O M E T H I N G G I R

116

I L I K E K I L L I N G P E O P L E
E B E C A U S E I T I S S O M U C
H F U N I T I S M O R E F U N T H
A N K I L L I N G W I L D G A M E
I N T H E F O R R E S T B E C A U
S E M A N I S T H E M O S T D A N
G E R O U E A N A M A L O F A L L
T O K I L L S O M E T H I N G G I K

E-BLOCK—7 (above)
  1. KLEIN
  2. L KANE

117

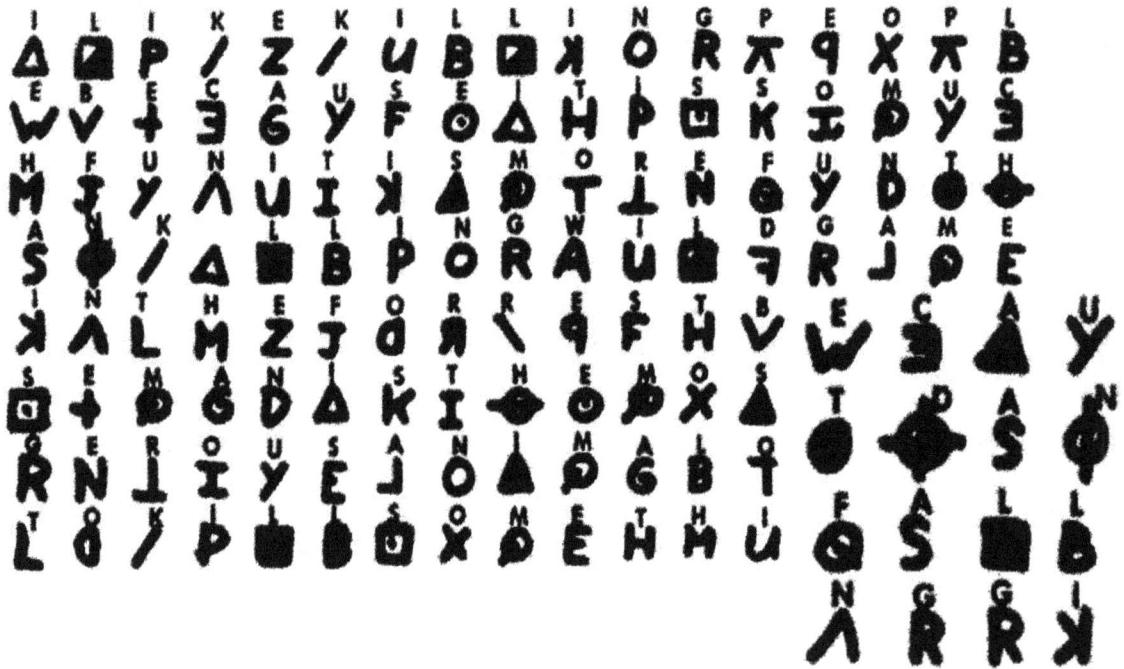

I LIKE KILLING PEOPLE

E-BLOCK—14

1. LARRY KLEIN
2. LARRY KANE
3. LARRY KING
4. L KAYE
5. LAWRENCE KAY
6. LAWRENCE K
7. THE ZODIAC SYMBOL

I L I K E K I L L I N G P E O P L

E B E C A U S E I T I S S O M U C

H F U N I T I S M O R E F U N T H

A N K I L L I N G W I L D G A M E

I N T H E F O R R E S T B E C A U

S E M A N I S T H E M O S T D A N

G E R O U E A N A M A L O F A L L

L O K I L L S O M E T H I N G G K

L K

Then, as shown earlier, he signs Z-136-A, the "Vallejo Times Herald Cipher," with his initials—LK—in the bottom left corner and bottom right corner—the two letters facing each other. These are the initials of LARRY KLEIN/KANE/ KAYE/ KING.

I L I K E K I L L I N G P E O P L
E B E C A U S E I T I S S O M U C
H F U N I T I S M O R E F U N T H
A N K I L L I N G W I L D G A M E
I N T H E F O R R E S T B E C A U
S E M A N I S T H E M O S T D A N
G E R O U E A N A M A L O F A L L
T O K I L L S O M E T H I N G G I

1. MY NAME IS...LARRY KLEIN
2. MY NAME IS...LARRY KANE
3. MY NAME IS...LARRY KING
4. MY NAME IS...LARRY K
5. LAWRENCE KAY
6. LAWRENCE K
7. THE ZODIAC SIGNATURE

As we have just seen, the ZODIAC signed the Z-136-A Cipher with his initials in the lower left and lower right corners facing one another—LK. He also signed the cipher with his four names in this last 4-by-4 block in the lower right corner. And he signed it with his Zodiac signature, the Circle Cross, as noted.

THE NAMES

OF THE

ZODIAC KILLER

REVEALED MULTIPLE TIMES

IN THE 'FINAL TEXT' OF

THE CIPHER

HE SENT TO THE

SAN FRANCISCO EXAMINER

JULY 31, 1969

"THE EXAMINER CIPHER"

Z-136-B

BLENDED TEXT

This is the cipher that was sent to the San Francisco Examiner. Once again, we see the Ciphertext paired together with the Plaintext.

Row 1 (plaintext): V E S M E T H E M O S T T H R I L

Row 2 (plaintext): L I N G E X P E R E N C E I T I S

Row 3 (plaintext): E V E N B E T T E R T H A N G E T

Row 4 (plaintext): T I N G Y O U R R O C K S O F F W

Row 5 (plaintext): I T H A G I R L T H E B E S T P A

Row 6 (plaintext): R T O F I T I S T H A T W H E N I

Row 7 (plaintext): D I E I W I L L B E R E B O R N I

Row 8 (plaintext): N P A R A D I C E A N D A L L T H

A-BLOCK—1 (above)
  1. KLEIN
  2. L KING

A-BLOCK—2 (below)
  1. KING

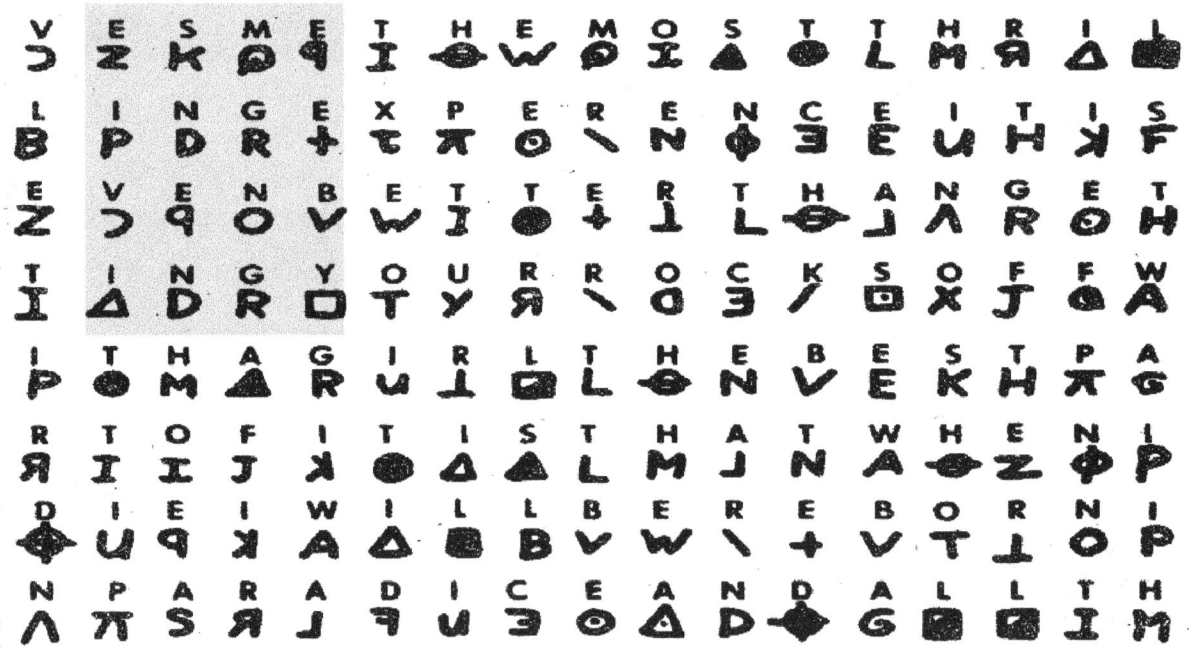

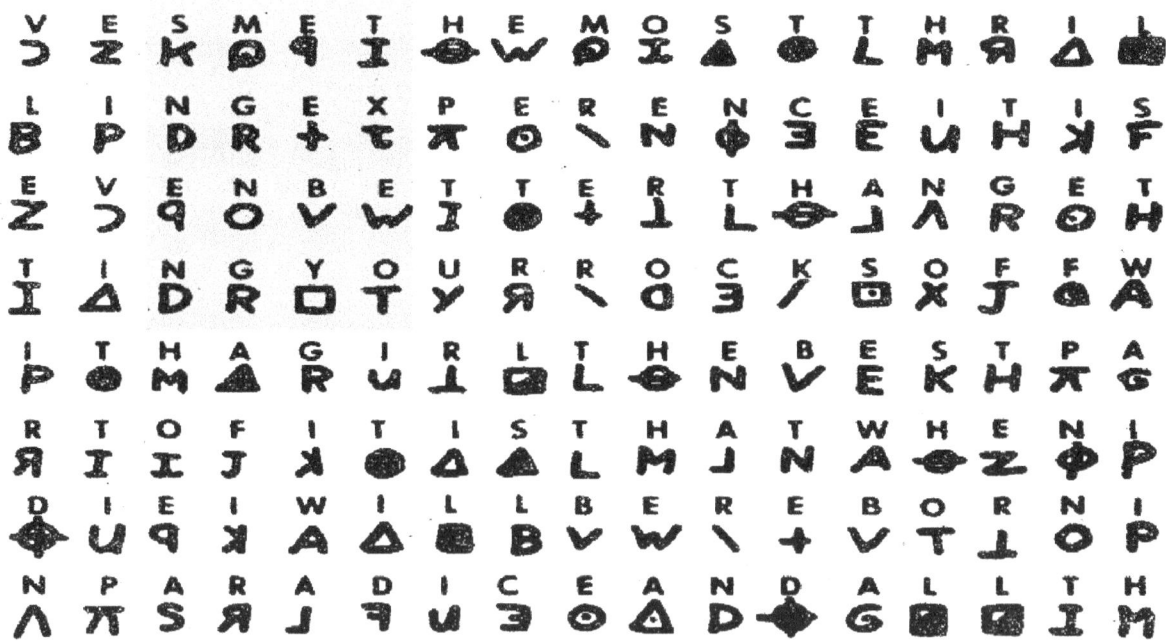

A-BLOCK—3 (above)
1. KING

A-BLOCK—4 (below)
1. KING

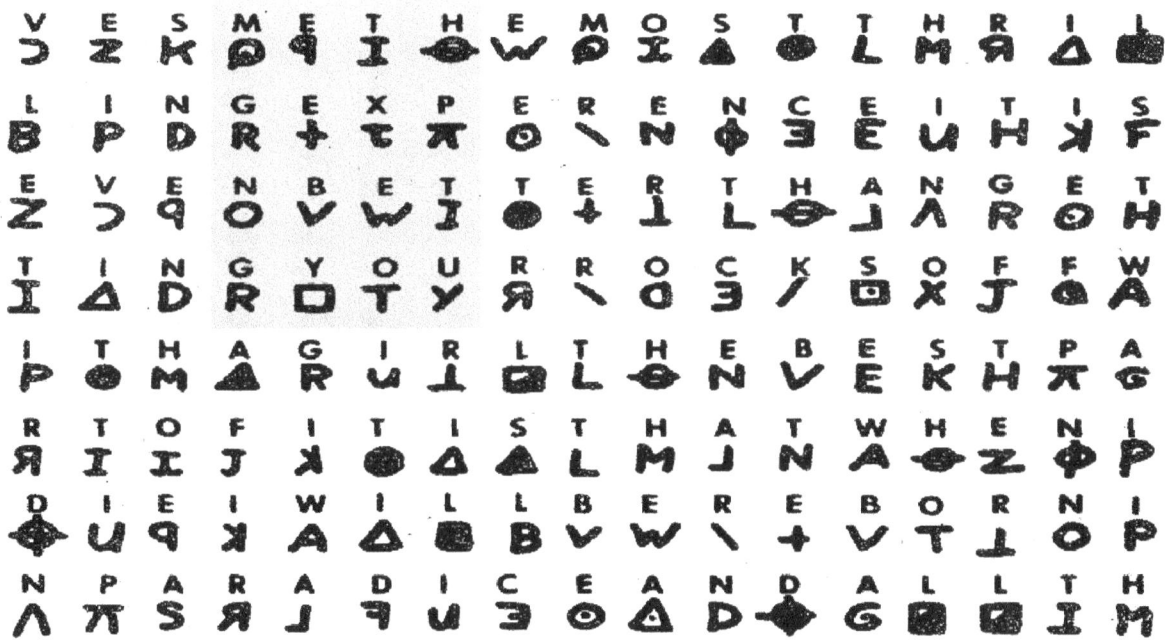

125

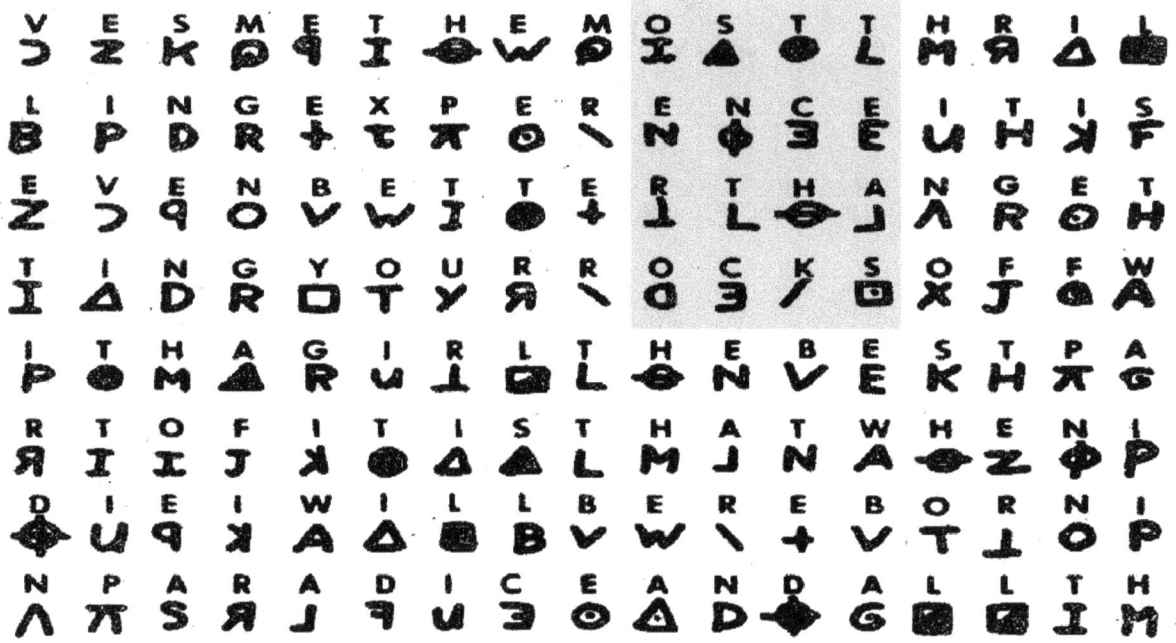

A-BLOCK—10 (above)
  1. L KANE

A-BLOCK—11 (below)
  1. L KLEIN
  2. L KANE

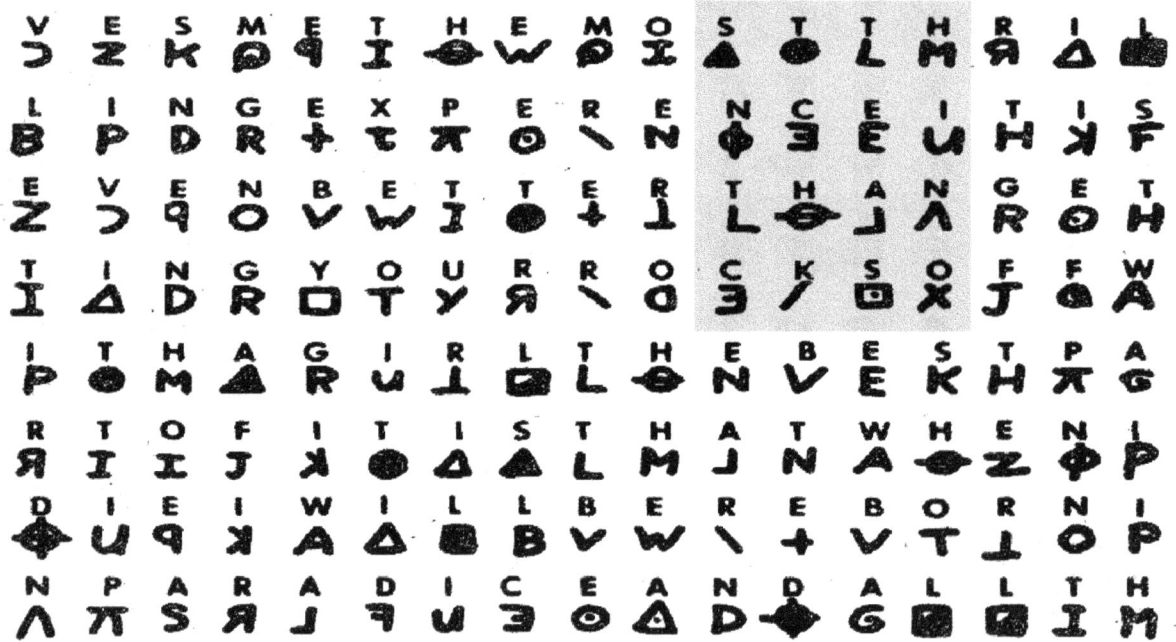

V E S M E T H E M O S T T H R I L

L I N G E X P E R E N C E I T I S

E V E N B E T T E R T H A N G E T H

I N G Y O U R R O C K S O F W A

I T H A G I R L T H E B E S T P A

R T O F I T I S T H A T W H E N I

D I E I W I L L B E R E B O R N I P

N P A R A D I C E A N D A L L T H I M

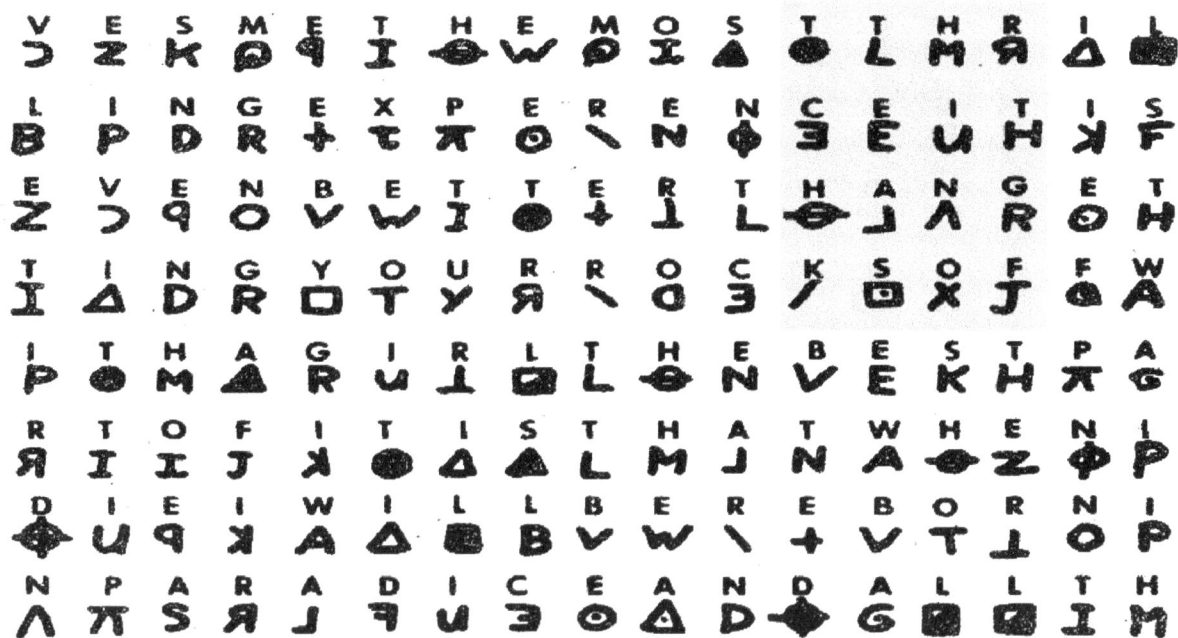

A-BLOCK—12 (above)
   1. L KLEIN
   2. L KANE
   3. L KING

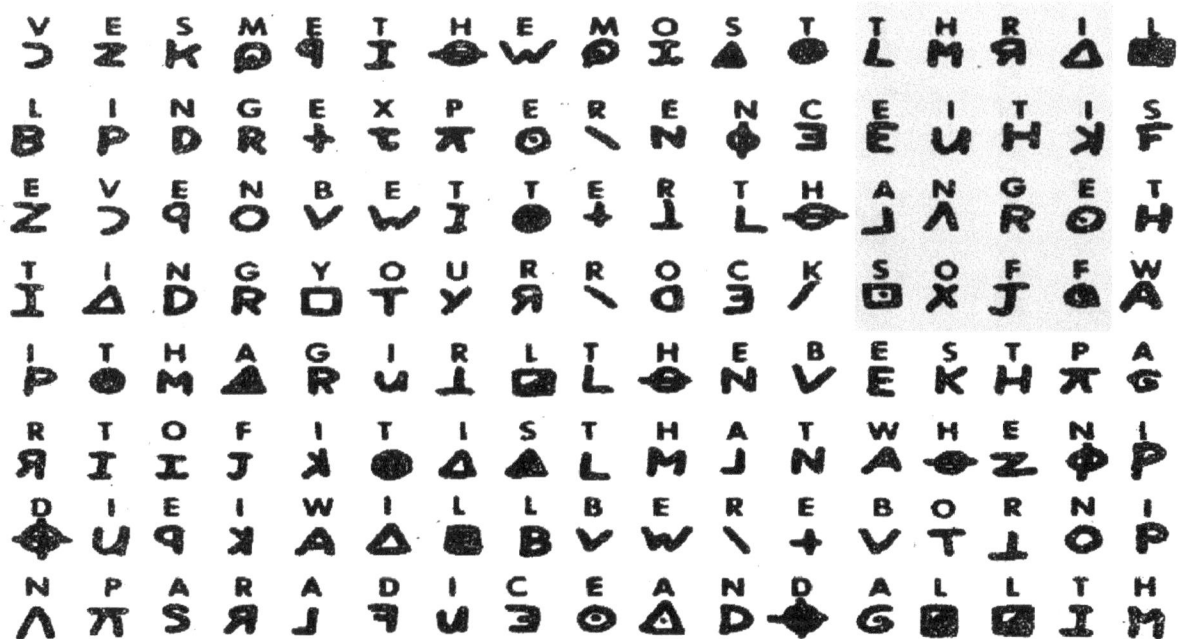

A-BLOCK—13 (below)
   1. L KLEIN
   2. L KANE
   3. L KING

V E S M E T H E M O S T T H R I L

L I N G E X P E R E N C E I T I S

E V E N B E T T E R T H A N G E T H

I N G Y O U R R O C K S O F W A

I T H A G I R L T H E B E S T P A

R T O F I T I S T H A T W H E N I

D I E I W I L L B E R E B O R N I P

N P A R A D I C E A N D A L L T H I M

127

V E S M E T H E M O S T T H R I L

L I N G E X P E R E N C E E I T I S

E V E N B E T T E R T H A N G E T

T I N G Y O U R R O C K S O F F W A

I T H A G I R L T H E B E S T P A G

R T O F I T I S T H A N T W H E N I

D I E I W I L L B E R E B O R N I P

N P A R A D I C E A N D A L L T H I M

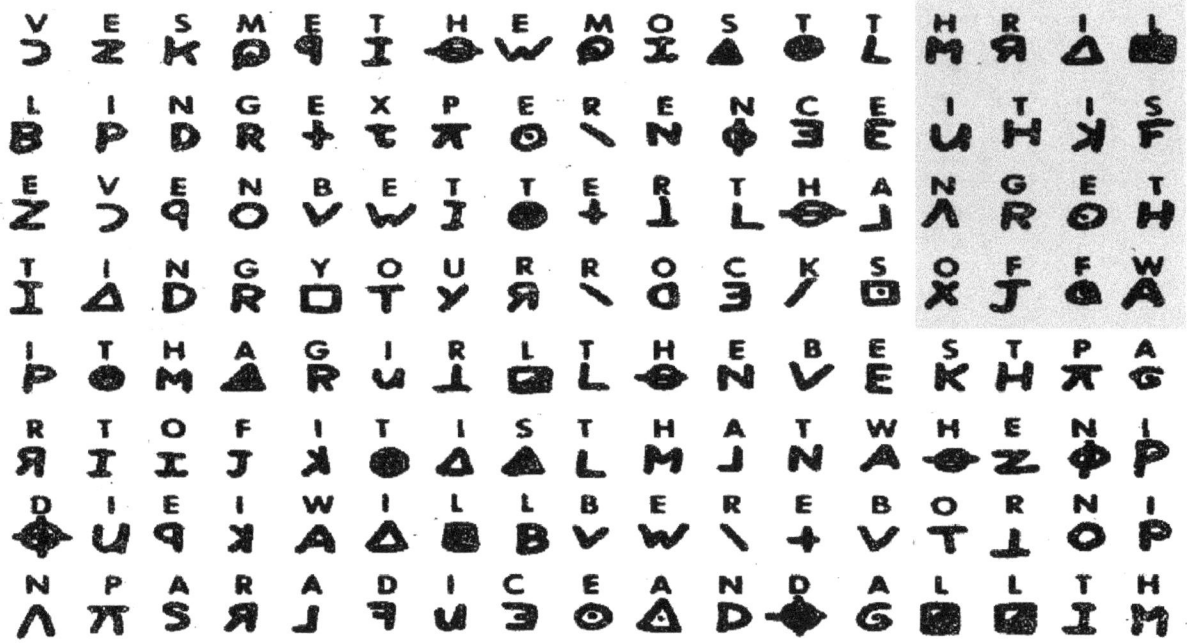

A-BLOCK—14 (above)
1. KLEIN
2. L KANE
3. L KING

B-BLOCK—4 (below)
1. KANE
2. KAYE
3. KING

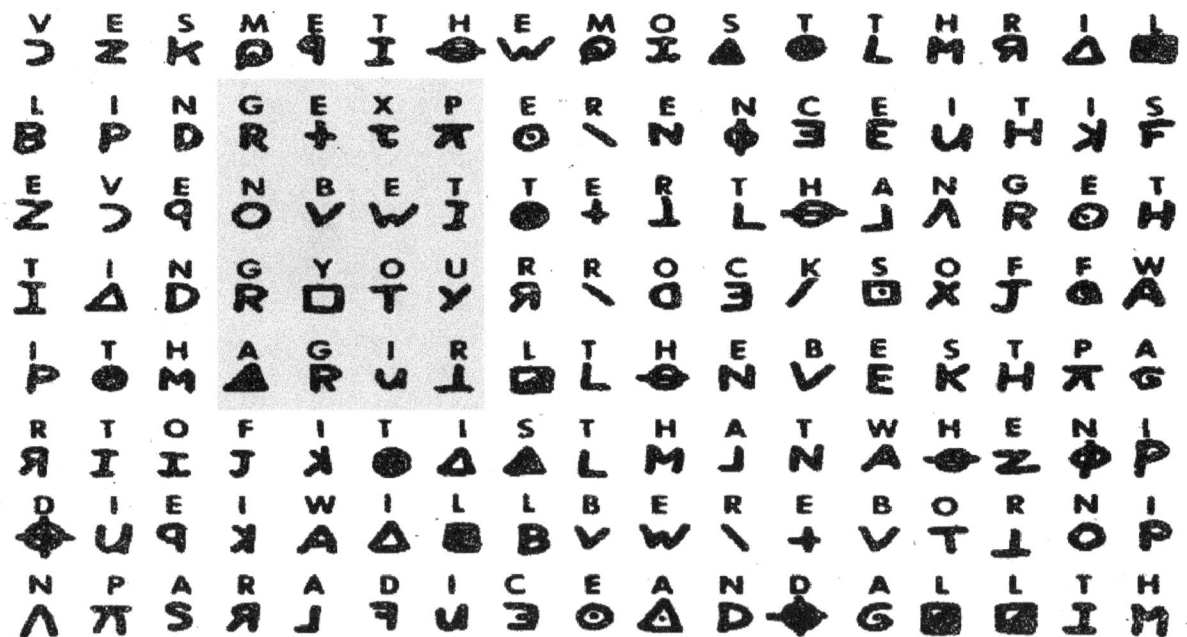

V E S M E T H E M O S T T H R I L

L I N G E X P E R E N C E E I T I S

E V E N B E T T E R T H A N G E T

T I N G Y O U R R O C K S O F F W A

I T H A G I R L T H E B E S T P A G

R T O F I T I S T H A N T W H E N I

D I E I W I L L B E R E B O R N I P

N P A R A D I C E A N D A L L T H I M

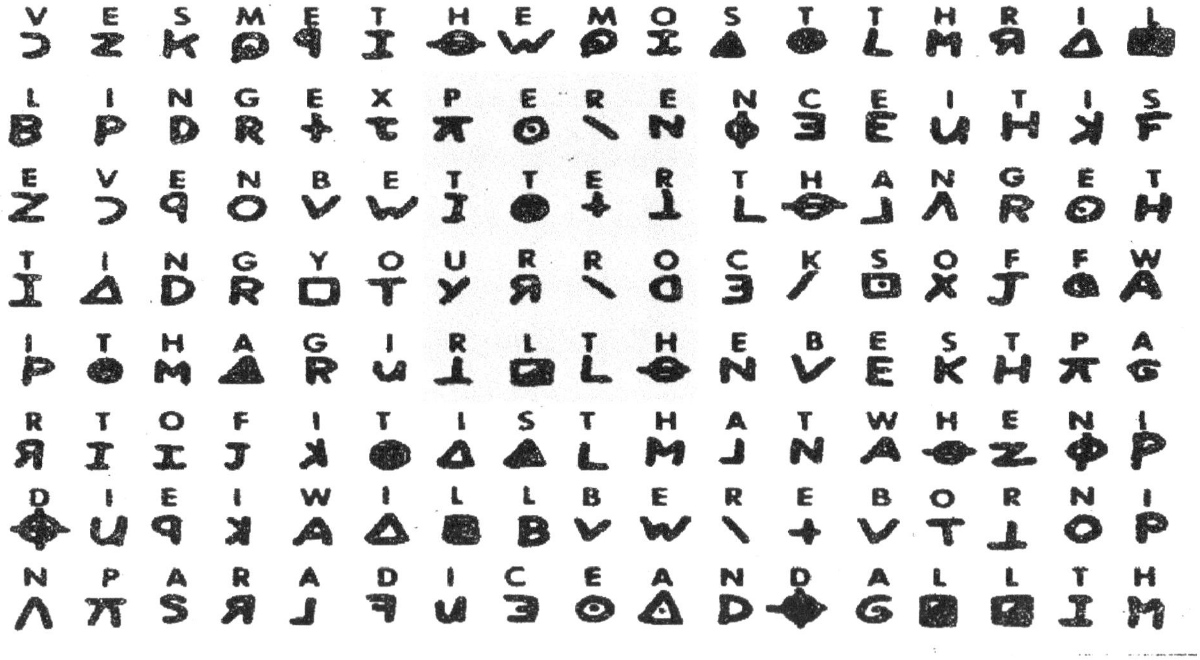

VESMETHEMOSTTHRILL
LINGEXPERENCEITIS
EVENBETTERTHANGETH
TINGYOURROCKSOFFWA
ITHAGIRLTHEBESTPAG
RTOFITISTHATWHENI
DIEIWILLBEREBORNI
NPARADICEANDALLTH

B-BLOCK—7 (above)
1. KLEIN

B-BLOCK—10 (below)
1. L KANE

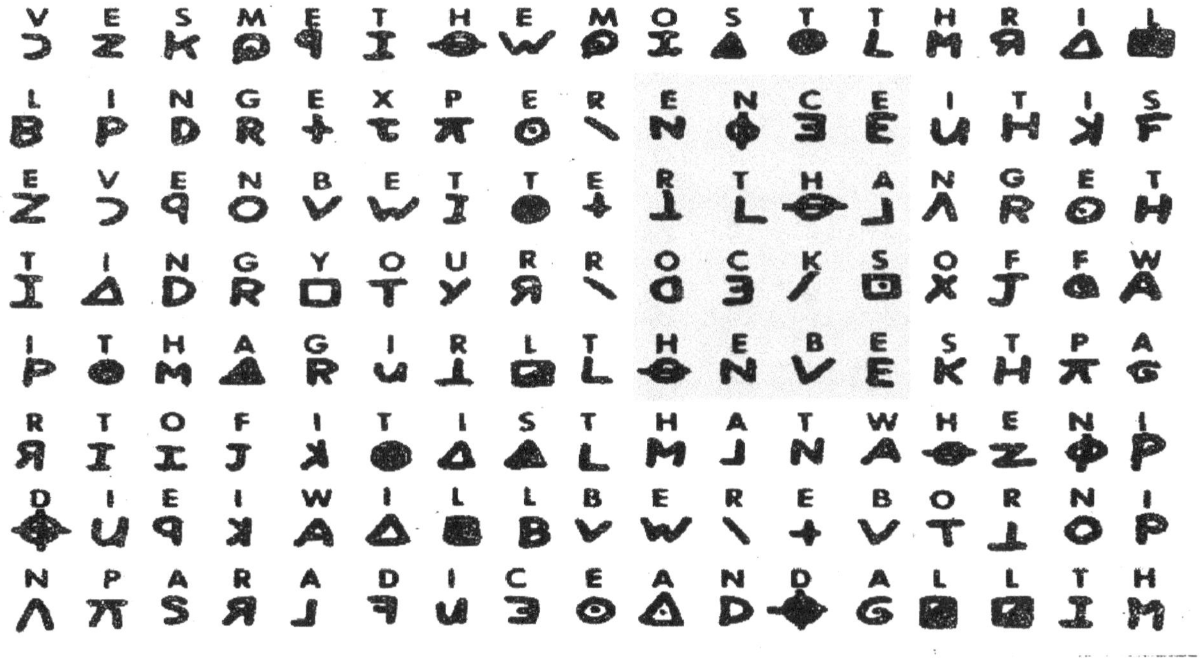

VESMETHEMOSTTHRILL
LINGEXPERENCEITIS
EVENBETTERTHANGETH
TINGYOURROCKSOFFWA
ITHAGIRLTHEBESTPAG
RTOFITISTHATWHENI
DIEIWILLBEREBORNI
NPARADICEANDALLTH

V E S M E T H E M O S T T H R I L
L I N G E X P E R E N C E I T I S
E V E N B E T T E R T H A N G E T H
I I N G Y O U R R O C K S O F F W A
I T H A G I R L T H E N V E K H P A
R T O F I T I S T H A T W H E N I
D I E I W I L L B E R E B O R N I P
N P A R A D I C E A N D A L L T H

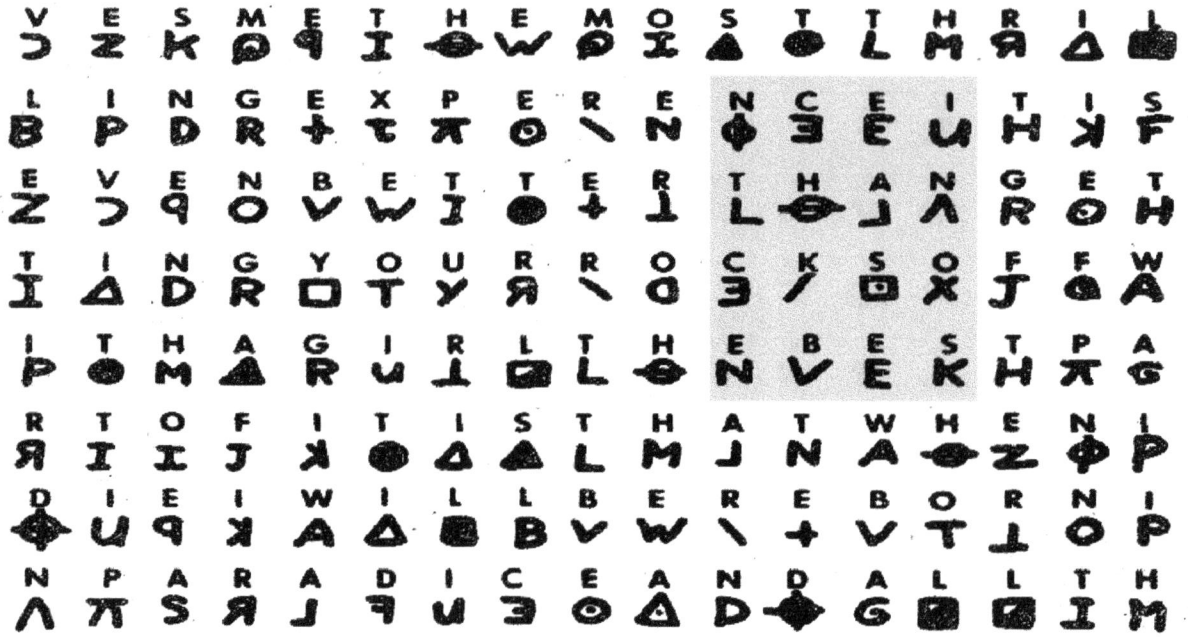

B-BLOCK—11 (above)
  1. L KLEIN
  2. L KANE

B-BLOCK—12 (below)
  1. KLEIN
  2. L KANE
  3. L KING

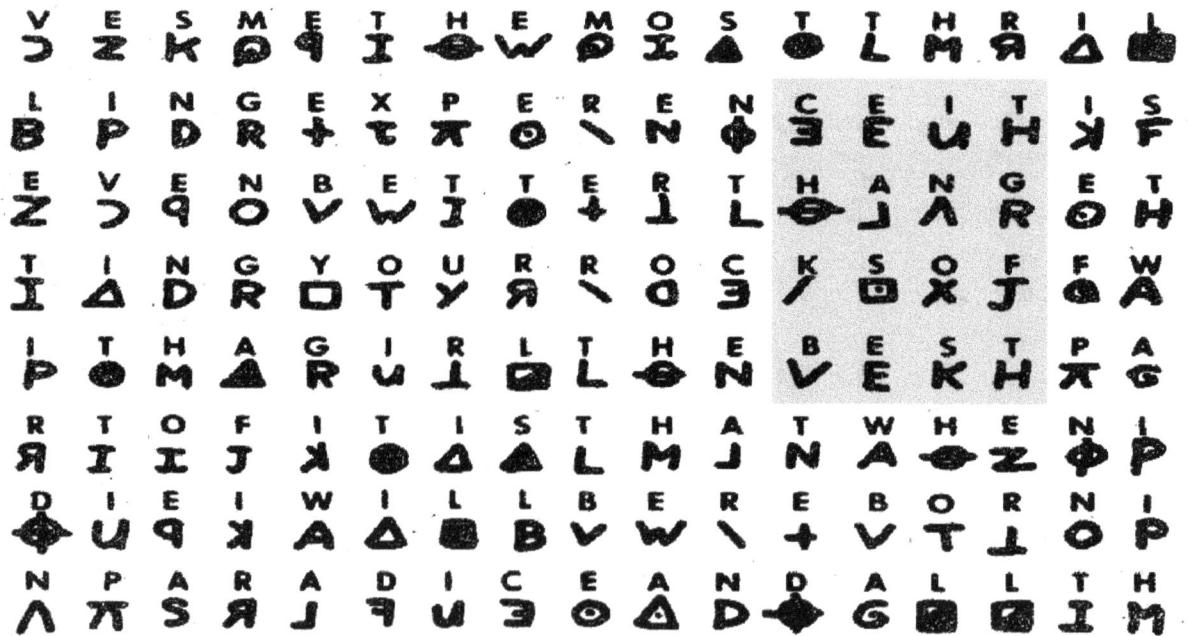

V E S M E T H E M O S T T H R I L
L I N G E X P E R E N C E I T I S
E V E N B E T T E R T H A N G E T H
I I N G Y O U R R O C K S O F F W A
I T H A G I R L T H E N V E K H P A
R T O F I T I S T H A T W H E N I
D I E I W I L L B E R E B O R N I P
N P A R A D I C E A N D A L L T H

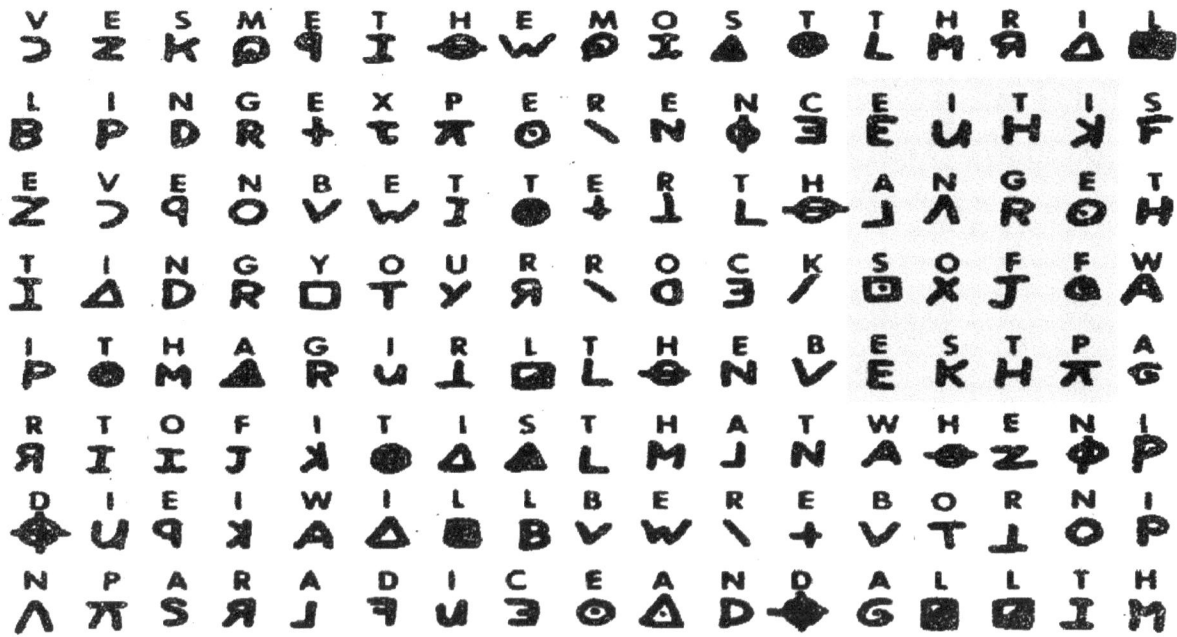

B-BLOCK—13 (above)
 1. KLEIN
 2. KANE
 3. KING

B-BLOCK—14 (below)
 1. KANE
 2. KING

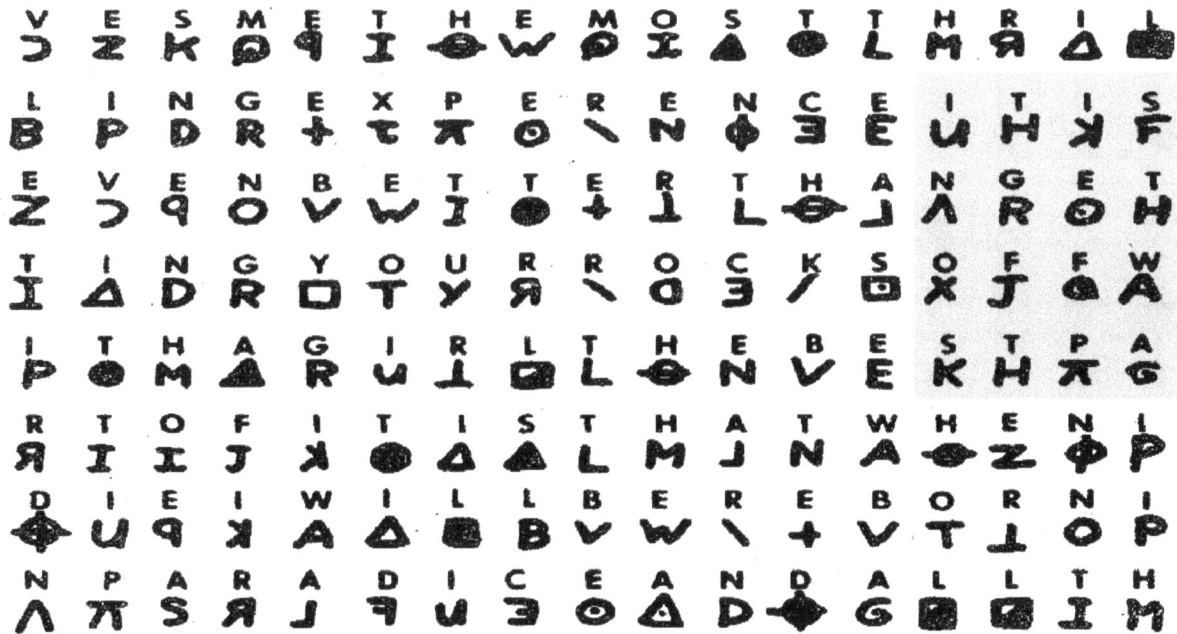

131

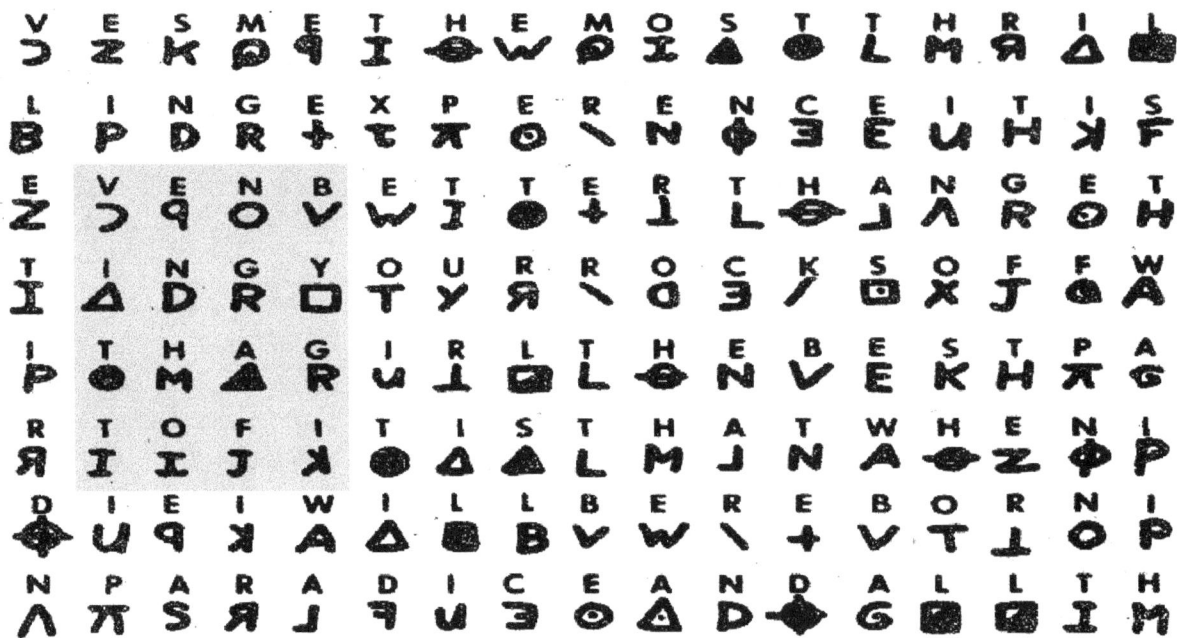

C-BLOCK—2 (above)
1. KAYE
2. KANE
3. KING

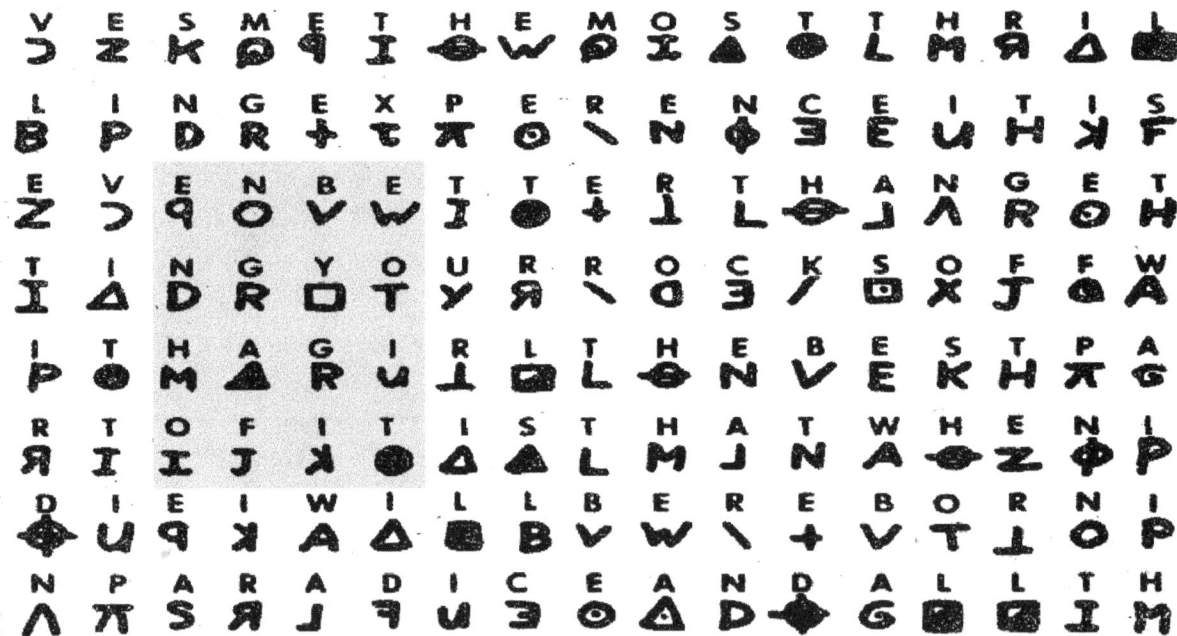

C-BLOCK—3 (below)
1. KAYE
2. KANE
3. KING

132

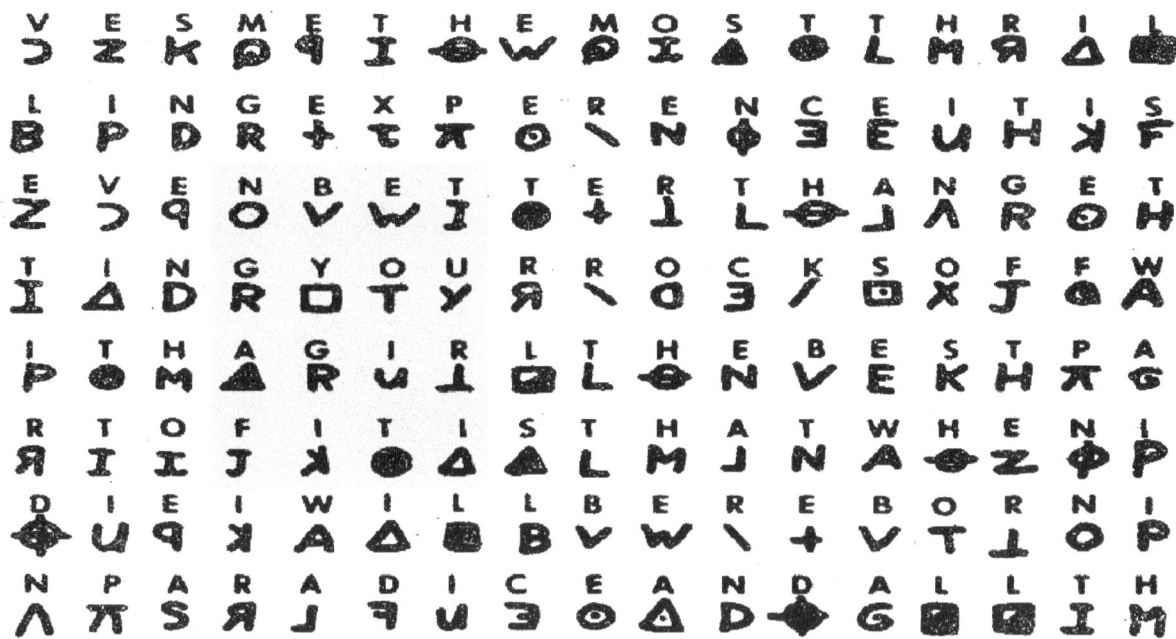

V E S M E T H E M O S T T H R I L
L I N G E X P E R E N C E I T I S
E V E N B E T T E R T H A N G E T H
I N G Y O U R R O C K S O F F W A
I T H A G I R L T H E B E S T P A G
R T O F I T I S T H A T W H E N I
D I E I W I L L B E R E B O R N I P
N P A R A D I C E A N D A L L T H

C-BLOCK—4 (above)
  1. KANE
  2. KAYE
  3. KING

C-BLOCK—9 (below)
  1. L KANE

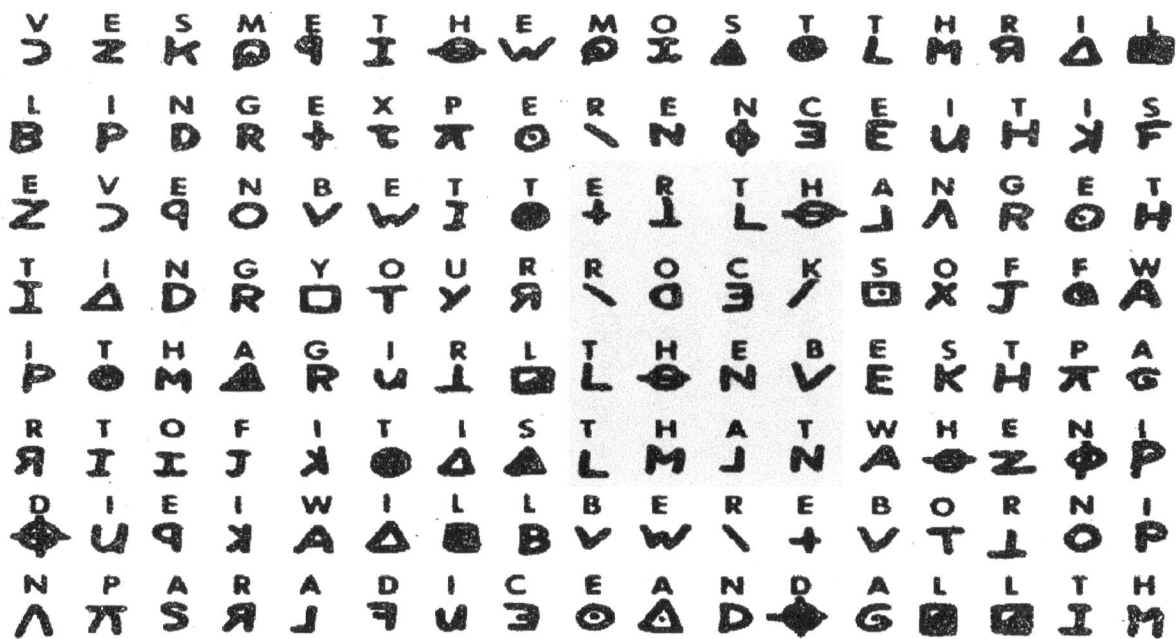

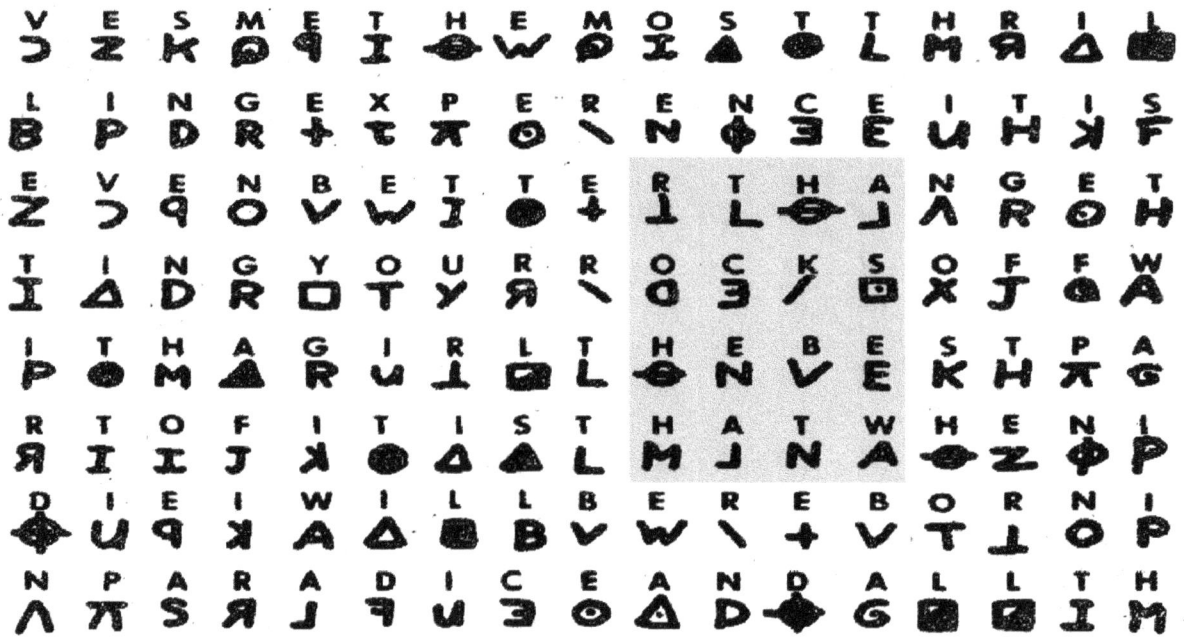

C-BLOCK—10 (above)
1. L KANE

C-BLOCK—11 (below)
1. L KANE

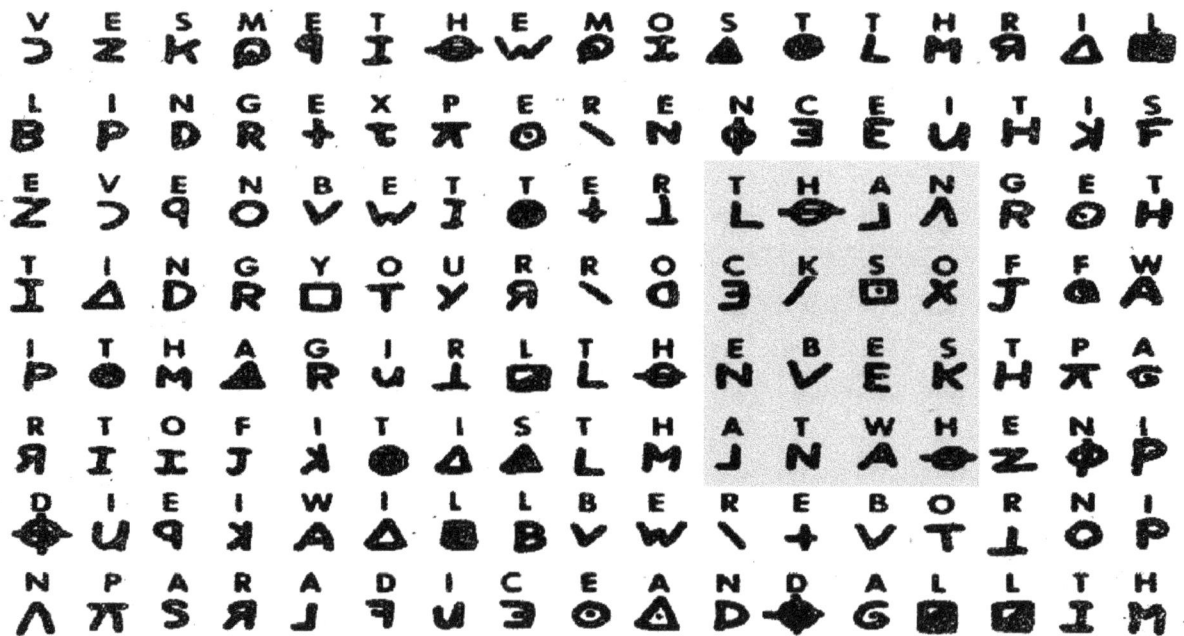

134

V E S M E T H E M O S T T H R I L L
L I N G E X P E R E N C E I T I S F
E V E N B E T T E R T H A N G E T H
I N G Y O U R R O C K S O F F W A
I T H A G I R L T H E B E S T P A G
R T O F I T I S T H A T W H E N N I
D I E I W I L L B E R E B O R N I P
N P A R A D I C E A N D A L L T H I M

C-BLOCK—12 (above)
  1. L KANE

C-BLOCK—13 (below)
  1. L KANE

V E S M E T H E M O S T T H R I L L
L I N G E X P E R E N C E I T I S F
E V E N B E T T E R T H A N G E T H
I N G Y O U R R O C K S O F F W A
I T H A G I R L T H E B E S T P A G
R T O F I T I S T H A T W H E N N I
D I E I W I L L B E R E B O R N I P
N P A R A D I C E A N D A L L T H I M

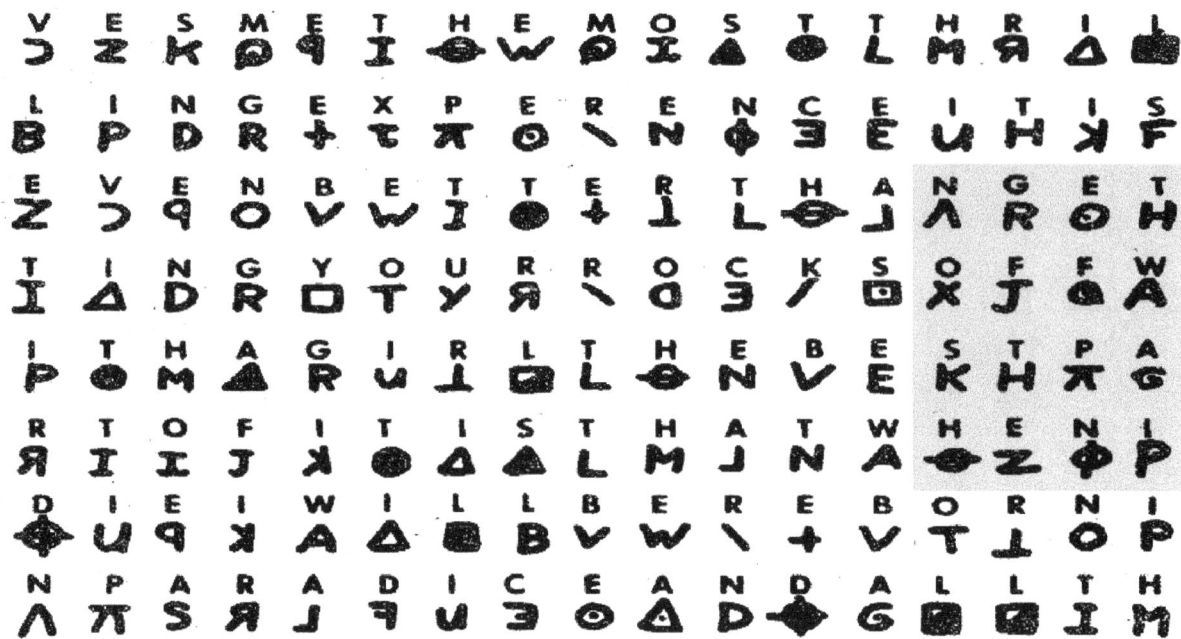

C-BLOCK—14 (above)
1. KANE
2. KING

D-BLOCK—1 (below)
1. KANE
2. KING

136

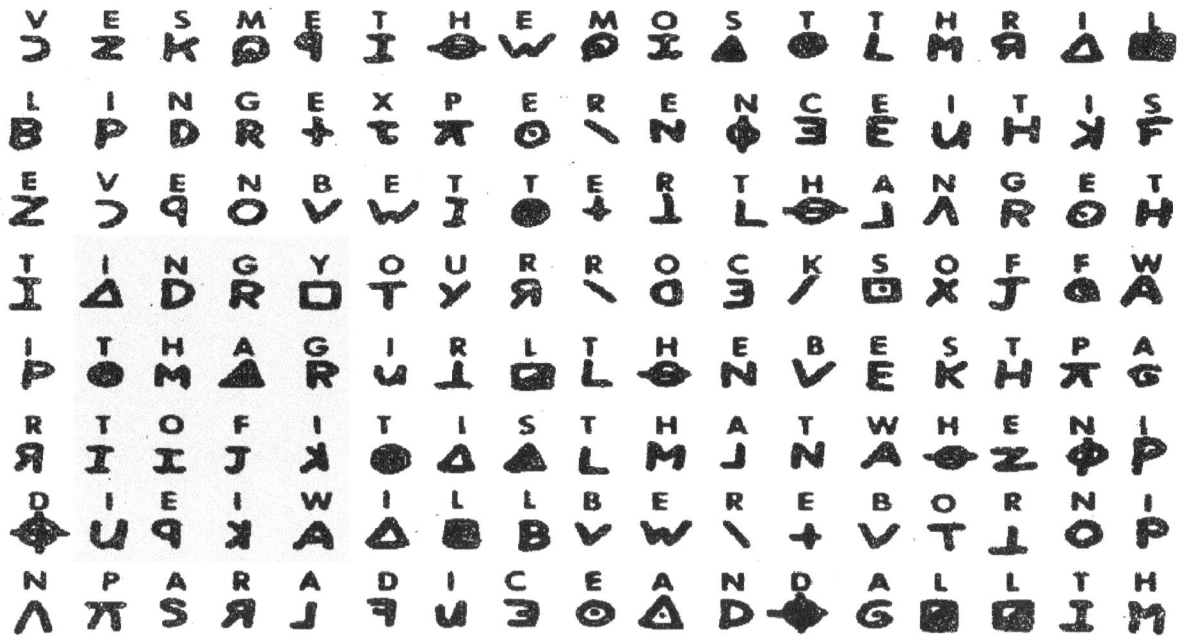

D-BLOCK—2 (above)

```
V  E  S  M  E  T  H  E  M  O  S  T  T  H  R  I  L
L  I  N  G  E  X  P  E  R  E  N  C  E  I  T  I  S  F
E  V  E  N  B  E  T  T  E  R  T  H  A  N  G  E  T  H
I  I  N  G  Y  O  U  R  R  O  C  K  S  O  F  F  W  A
P  I  T  H  A  G  I  R  L  T  H  E  B  E  S  T  P  A
R  T  O  F  I  T  I  S  T  H  A  T  W  H  E  N  I
D  I  E  I  W  I  L  L  B  E  R  E  B  O  R  N  I  P
N  P  A  R  A  D  I  C  E  A  N  D  A  L  L  T  H
```

D-BLOCK—2 (above)
  1. KANE
  2. KING
  3. KAYE

D-BLOCK—3 (below)
  1. KANE
  2. KAYE
  3. KING

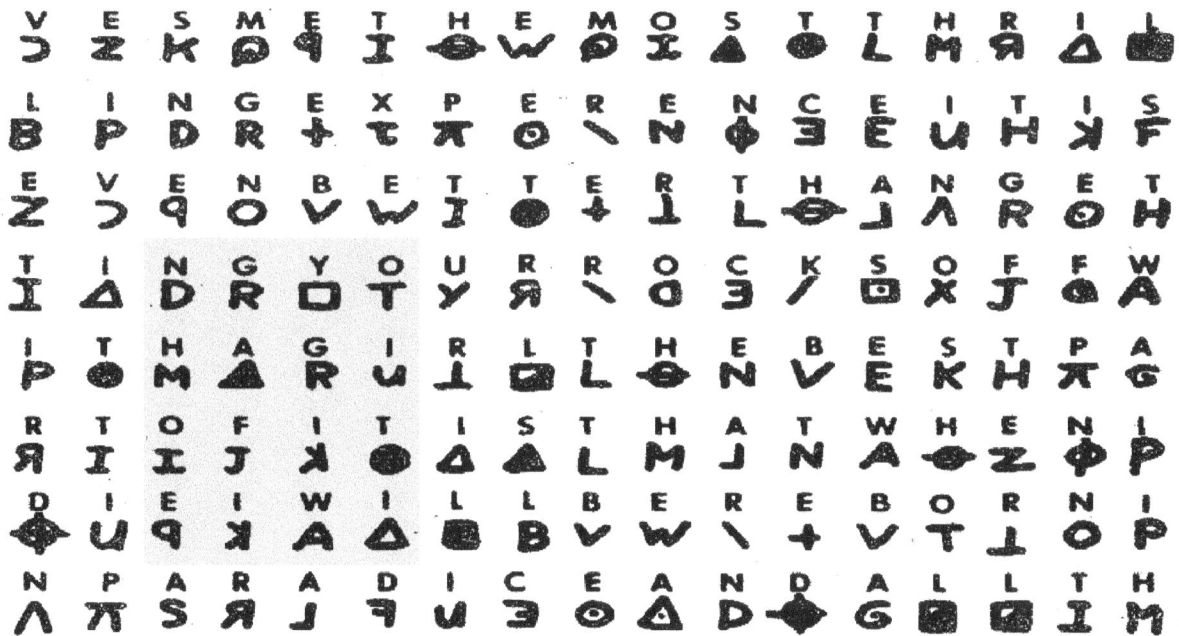

```
V  E  S  M  E  T  H  E  M  O  S  T  T  H  R  I  L
L  I  N  G  E  X  P  E  R  E  N  C  E  I  T  I  S  F
E  V  E  N  B  E  T  T  E  R  T  H  A  N  G  E  T  H
I  I  N  G  Y  O  U  R  R  O  C  K  S  O  F  F  W  A
P  I  T  H  A  G  I  R  L  T  H  E  B  E  S  T  P  A
R  T  O  F  I  T  I  S  T  H  A  T  W  H  E  N  I
D  I  E  I  W  I  L  L  B  E  R  E  B  O  R  N  I  P
N  P  A  R  A  D  I  C  E  A  N  D  A  L  L  T  H
```

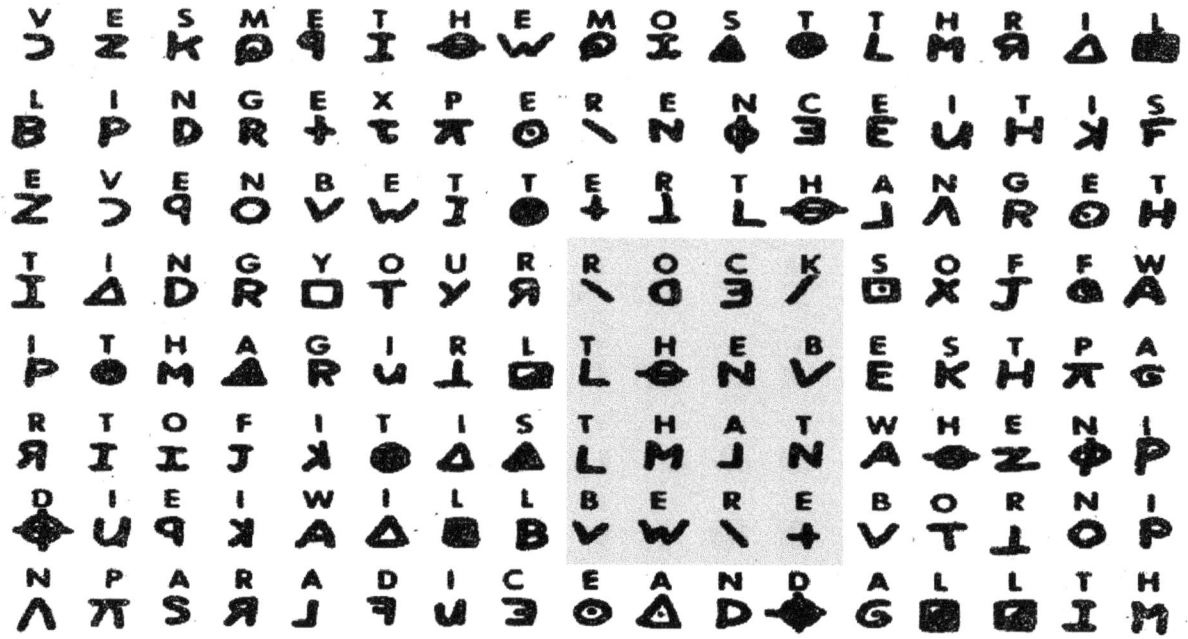

D-BLOCK—9 (above)
1. L KANE

D-BLOCK—10 (below)
1. L KANE

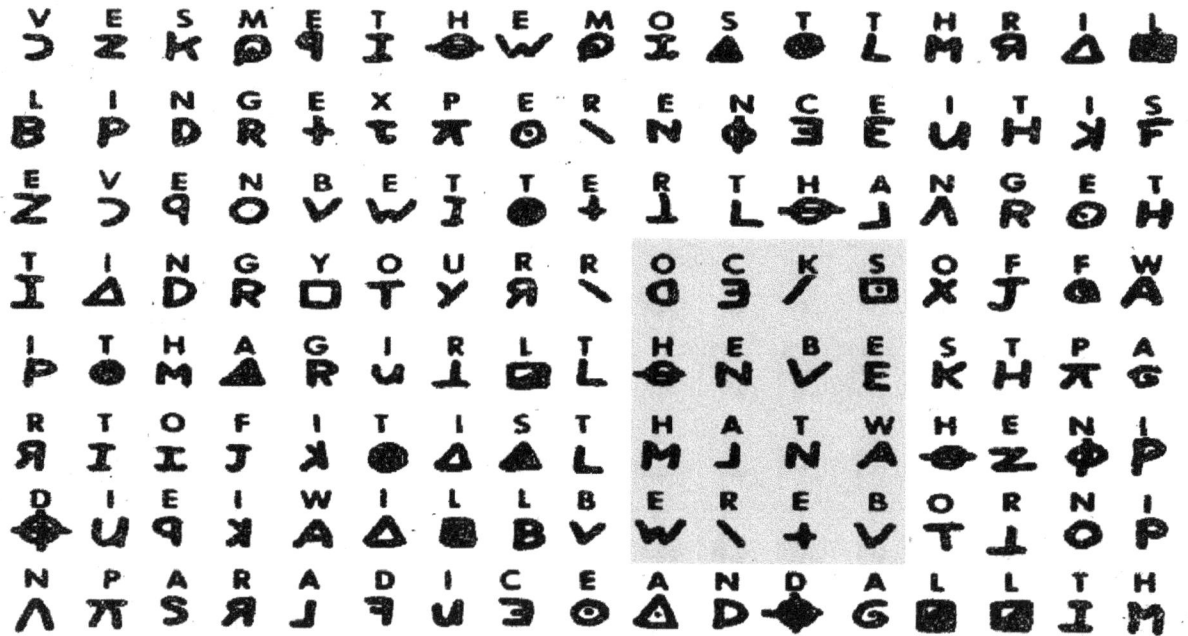

V E S M E T H E M O S T T H R I L
L I N G E X P E R E N C E I T I S
E V E N B E T T E R T H A N G E T
T I N G Y O U R R O C K S O F F W A
I T H A G I R L T H E B E S T P A
R T O F I T I S T H A T W H E N I
D I E I W I L L B E R E B O R N I
N P A R A D I C E A N D A L L T H

D-BLOCK—11 (above)
1. L KANE

D-BLOCK—12 (below)
1. KANE

V E S M E T H E M O S T T H R I L
L I N G E X P E R E N C E I T I S
E V E N B E T T E R T H A N G E T
T I N G Y O U R R O C K S O F F W A
I T H A G I R L T H E B E S T P A
R T O F I T I S T H A T W H E N I
D I E I W I L L B E R E B O R N I
N P A R A D I C E A N D A L L T H

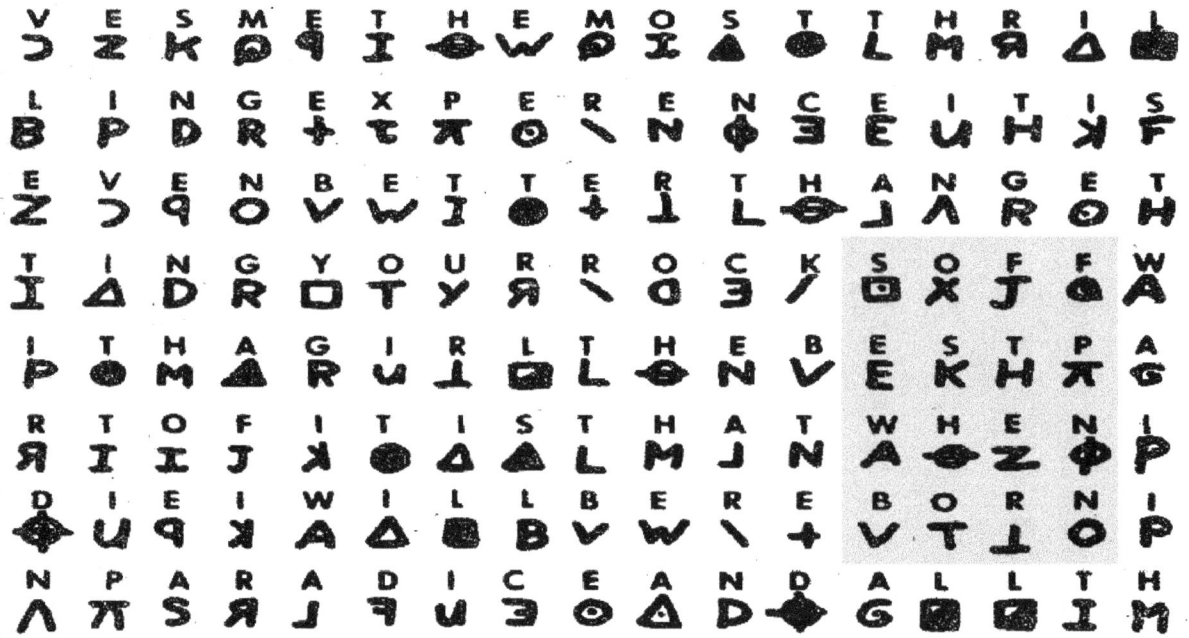

D-BLOCK—13 (above)
1. KANE

D-BLOCK—14 (below)
1. KANE

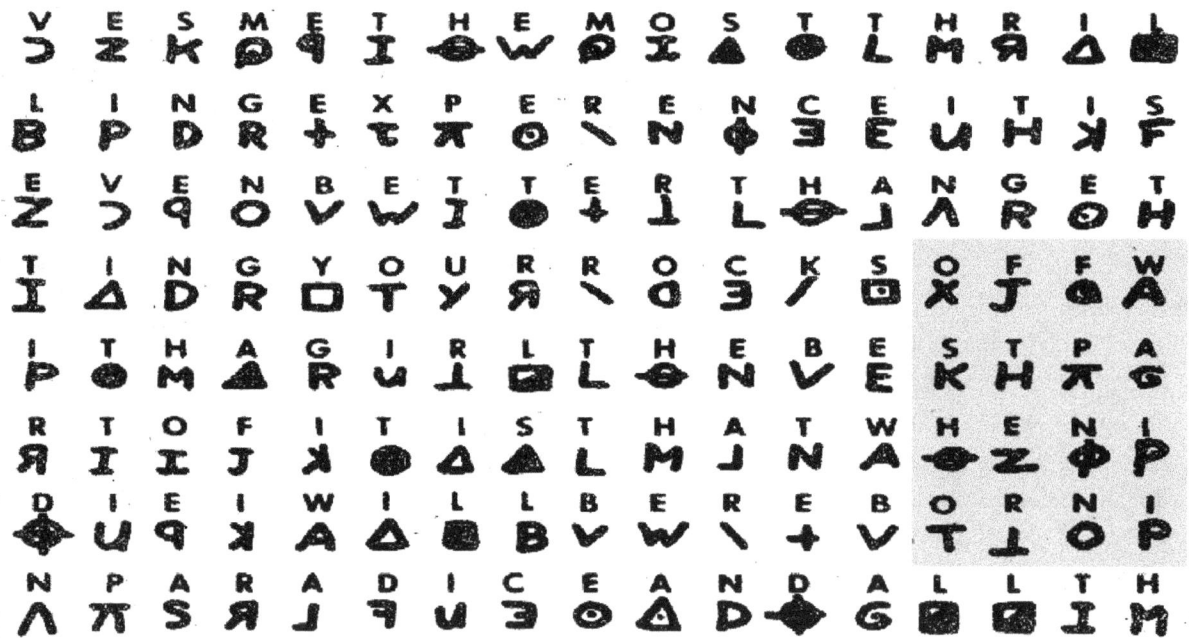

V E S M E T H E M O S T T H R I L
L I N G E X P E R E N C E I T I S
E V E N B E T T E R T H A N G E T
I I N G Y O U R R O C K S O F F W
I T H A G I R L T H E B E S T P A
R T O F I T I S T H A T W H E N I
D I E I W I L L B E R E B O R N I
N P A R A D I C E A N D A L L T H

E-BLOCK—1 (above)   E-BLOCK—11 (below)
  1. KANE   1. L KANE

V E S M E T H E M O S T T H R I L
L I N G E X P E R E N C E I T I S
E V E N B E T T E R T H A N G E T
I I N G Y O U R R O C K S O F F W
I T H A G I R L T H E B E S T P A
R T O F I T I S T H A T W H E N I
D I E I W I L L B E R E B O R N I
N P A R A D I C E A N D A L L T H

E-BLOCK—12 (above)
  1. L KANE

E-BLOCK—13 (below)
  1. L KANE
  2. L KING

V E S M E T H E M O S T T H R I L
L I N G E X P E R E N C E I T I S
E V E N B E T T E R T H A N G E T
T I N G Y O U R R O C K S O F F W A
I T H A G I R L T H E B E S T P A
R T O F I T I S T H A T W H E N I
D I E I W I L L B E R E B O R N I
N P A R A D I C E A N D A L L T H

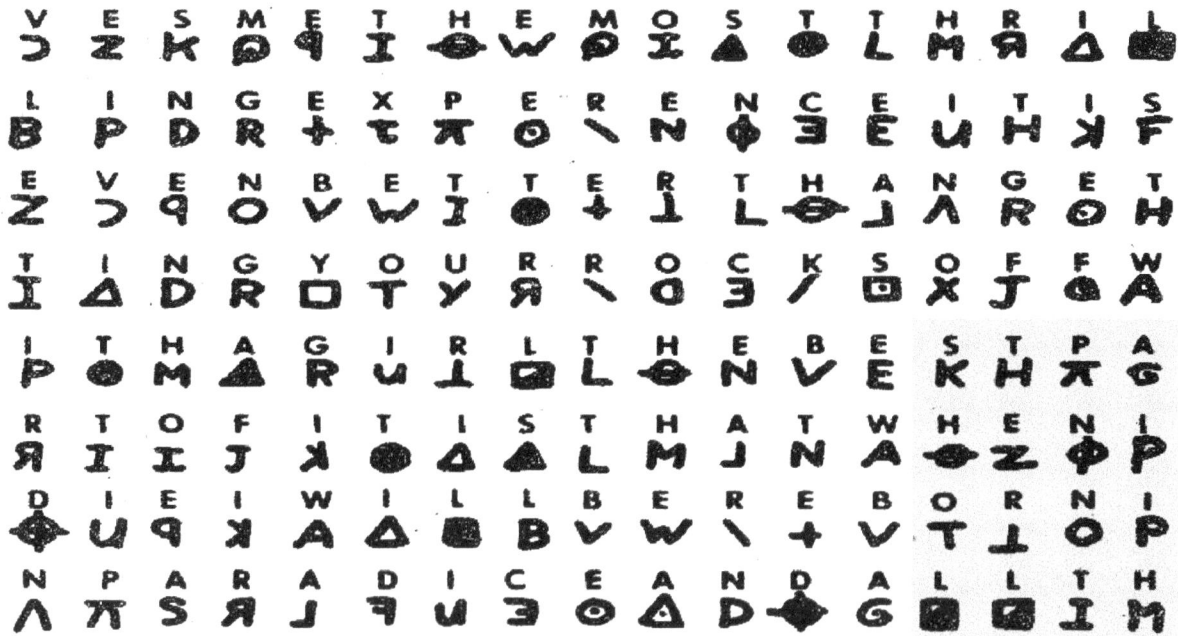

E-BLOCK—14 (above)
1. I AM L KLEIN
2. I'M L KANE
3. I AM L KING
4. I AM THE Z

THE NAMES

OF THE

ZODIAC KILLER

REVEALED MULTIPLE TIMES

IN THE 'FINAL TEXT' OF

THE CIPHER

HE SENT TO THE

SAN FRANCISCO CHRONICLE

JULY 31, 1969

"THE CHRONICLE CIPHER"

Z-136-C

BLENDED TEXT

This is the cipher that was sent to the San Francisco Chronicle. We see the Ciphertext is paired together with the Plaintext.

E I H A V E K I L L E D W I L L B
E C O M E M Y S L A V E S I W I L L
L N O T G I V E Y O U M Y N A M E
B E C A U S E Y O U W I L L T R Y
T O S L O I D O W N O R S T O P M
Y C O L L E C T I N G O F S L A V
E S F O R M Y A F T E R L I F E E
B E O R I E T E M E T H H P I T I

E I H A V E K I L L E D W I L L B
E C O M E M Y S L A V E S I W I L
L N O T G I V E Y O U M Y N A M E
B E C A U S E Y O U W I L L T R Y
T O S L O I D O W N O R S T O P M
Y C O L L E C T I N G O F S L A V
E S F O R M Y A F T E R L I F E E
B E O R I E T E M E T H H P I T I

A-BLOCK—1 (above)

1. KLEIN
2. L KANE
3. L KING

A-BLOCK—2 (below)

1. KANE
2. KAYE
3. KING

E I H A V E K I L L E D W I L L B
E C O M E M Y S L A V E S I W I L
L N O T G I V E Y O U M Y N A M E
B E C A U S E Y O U W I L L T R Y
T O S L O I D O W N O R S T O P M
Y C O L L E C T I N G O F S L A V
E S F O R M Y A F T E R L I F E E
B E O R I E T E M E T H H P I T I

A-BLOCK—3 (above)
1. KAYE
2. "I AM CAUGHT"
3. "YOU'VE CAUGHT ME"
4. "YOU GOT ME"

A-BLOCK—4 (below)
1. KAYE

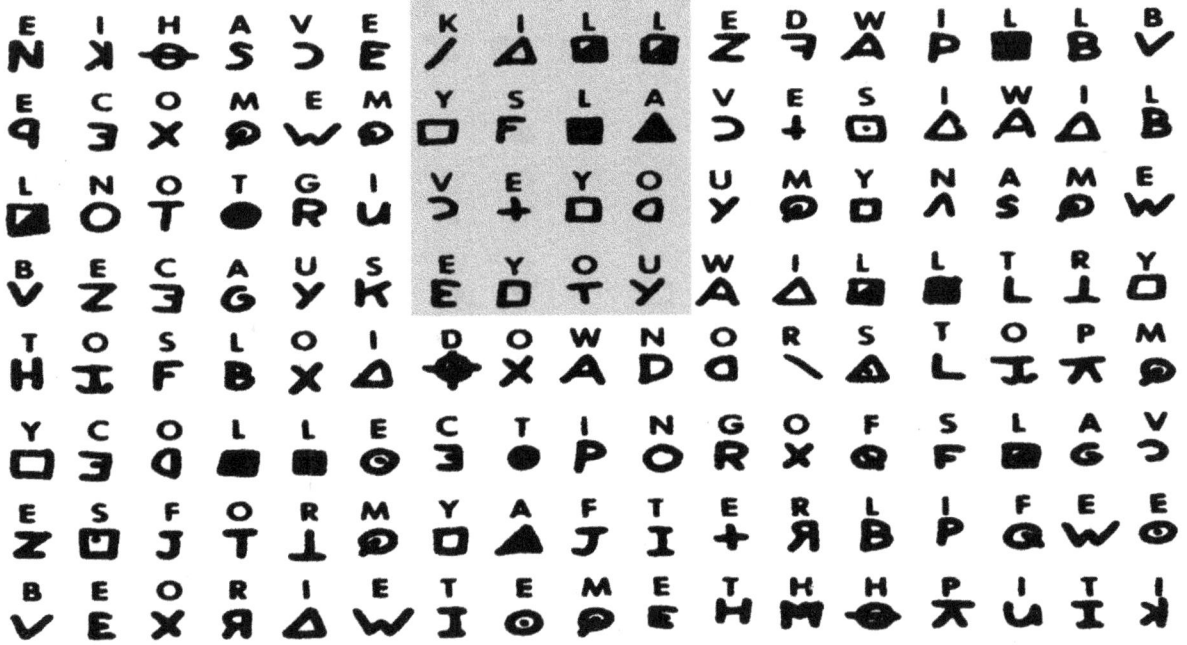

A-BLOCK—7 (above)
1. L KAYE
2. "I'LL SLAY YOU"

B-BLOCK—3 (below)
1. L KAYE

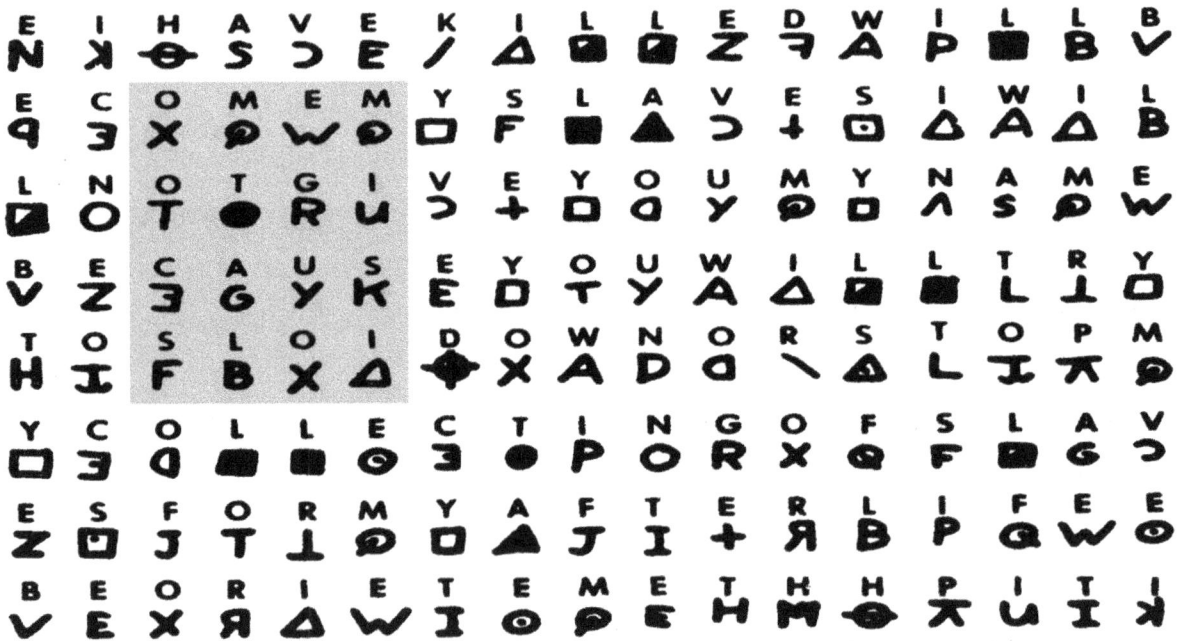

B-BLOCK—4 (above)
  1. L KAYE

B-BLOCK—6 (below)
  1. L KAYE

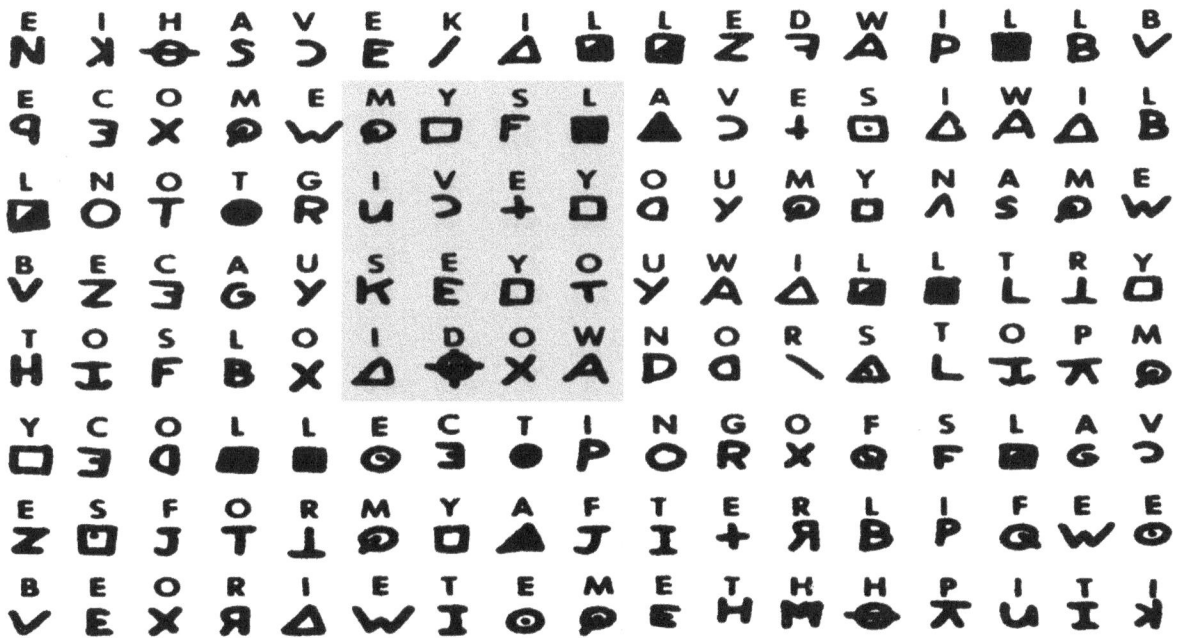

151

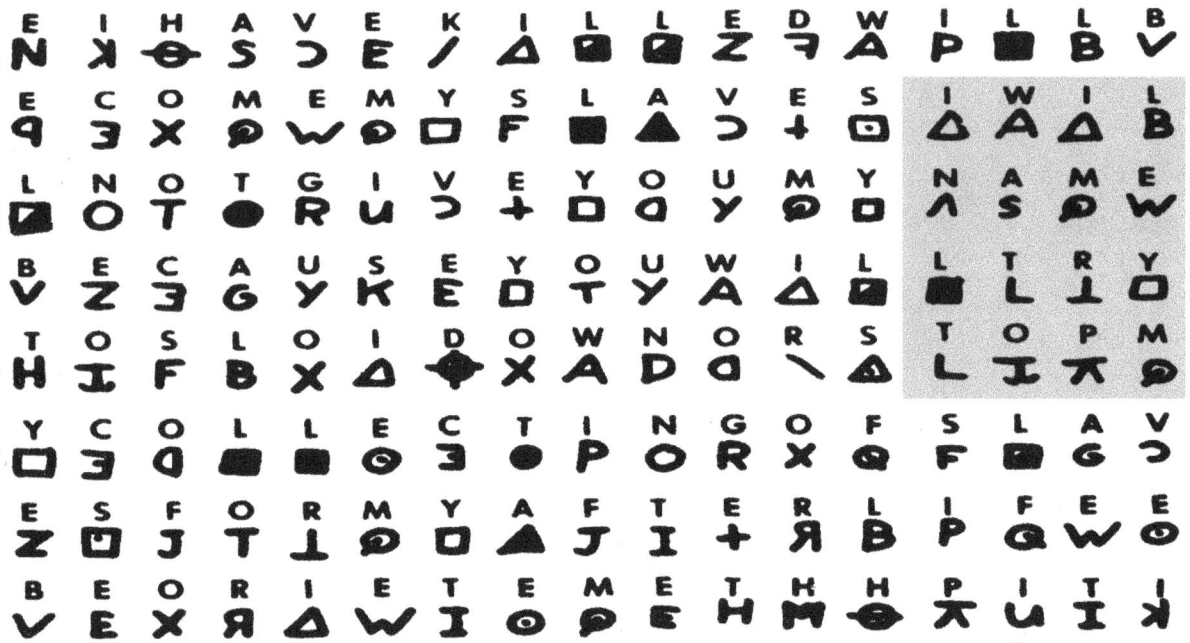

B-BLOCK—14 (above)
1. L KLEIN
2. L KAYE
3. L KANE

C-BLOCK—3 (below)
1. L KAYE

152

C-BLOCK—4 (above)
1. L KAYE

C-BLOCK—6 (below)
1. KAYE

153

C-BLOCK—14 (above)
  1. L KAYE
  2. L KANE

D-BLOCK—3 (below)
  1. L KAYE

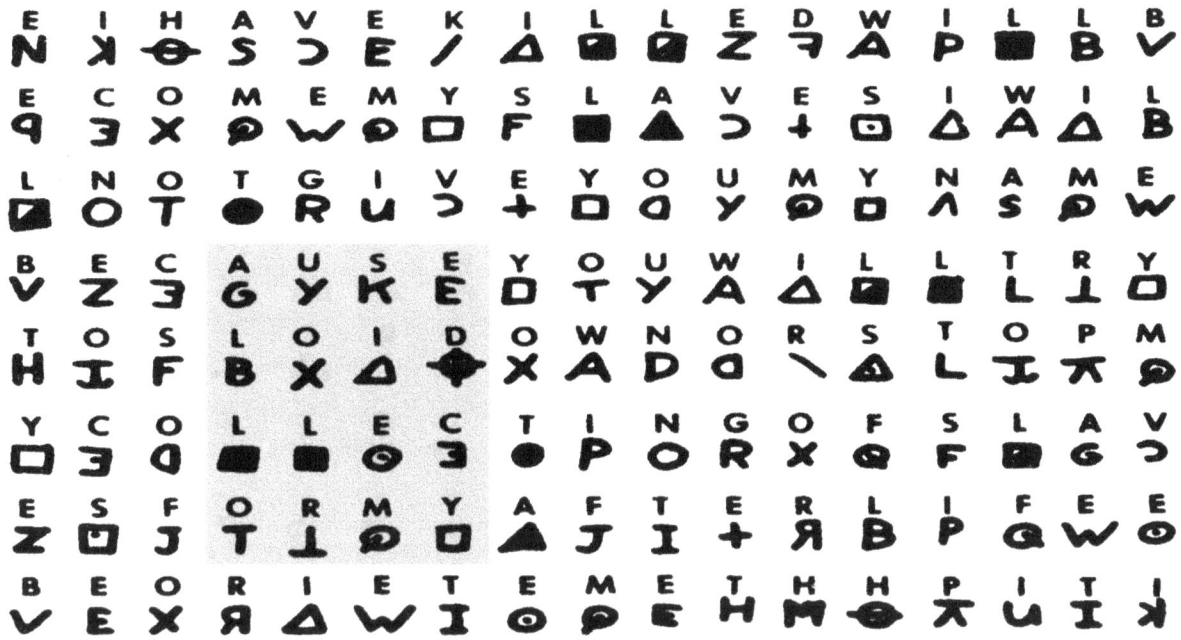

D-BLOCK—4 (above)
  1. L KAYE

D-BLOCK—5 (below)
  1. L KAYE

155

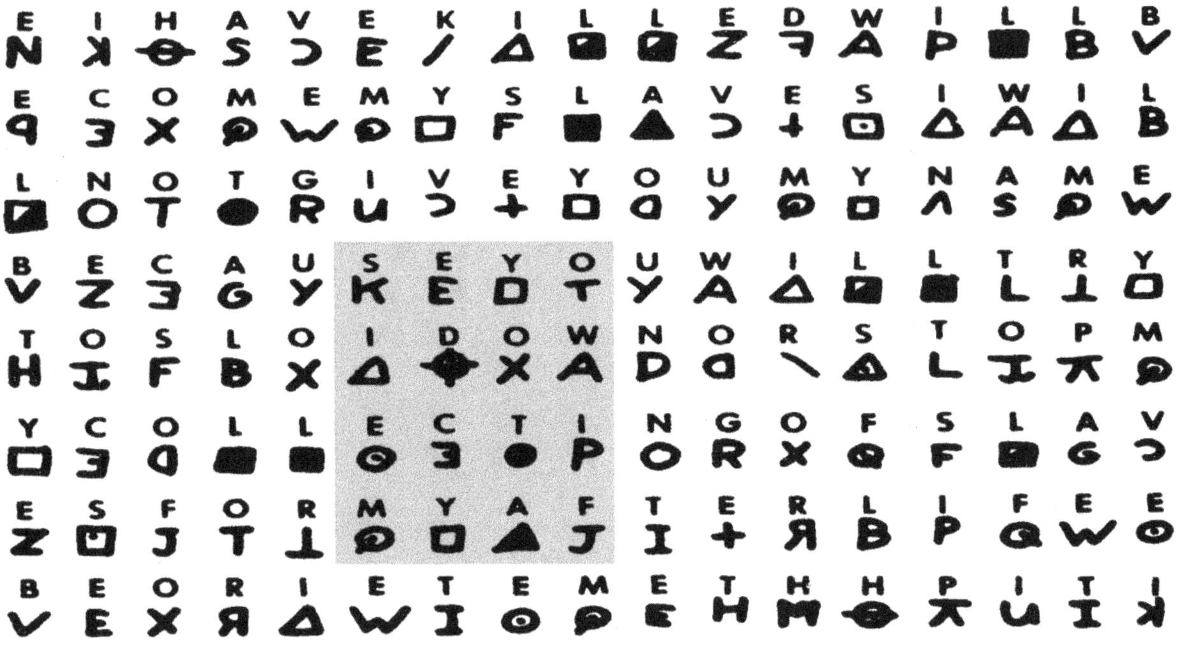

D-BLOCK—6 (above)
1. KAYE

D-BLOCK—14 (below)
1. L KAYE

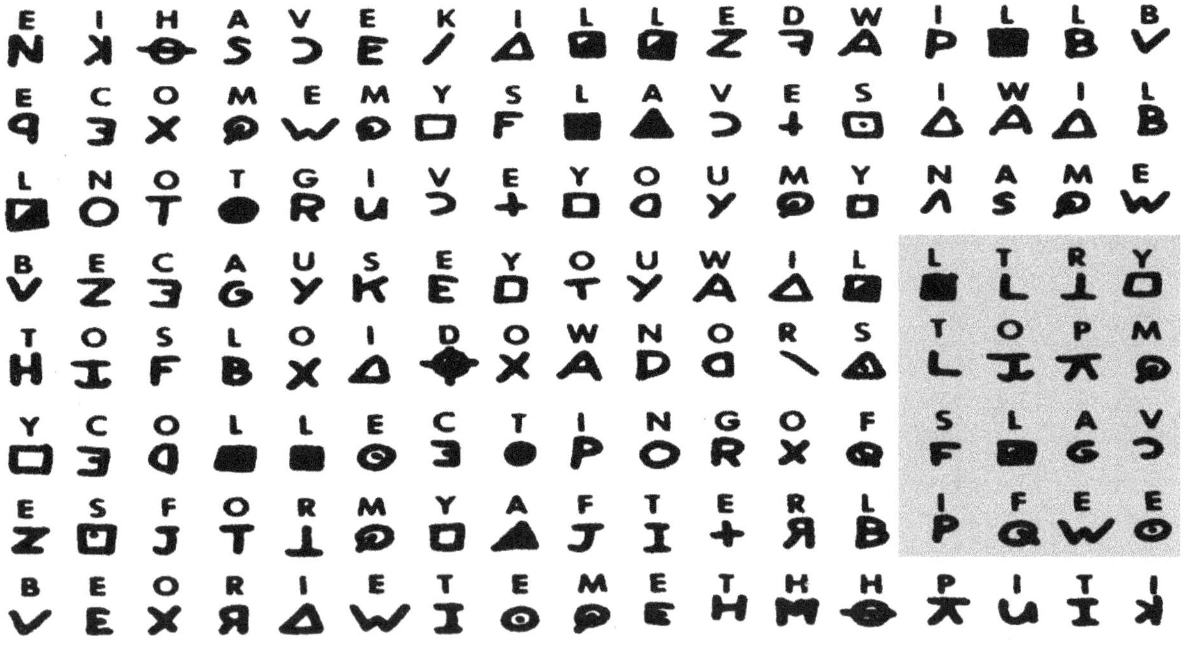

In the last of the three ciphers the Zodiac sent to the three newspapers on July 31, 1969, he gives us his initials. Let us look closer to see how he ends the Z-408 or what I call the Z-136-C—the "Chronicle Cipher."

E I H A V E K I L L E D W I L L B
N K ⊙ S Ɔ E ╱ Δ ■ ■ Z Ⴑ A P ■ B V

E C O M E M Y S L A V E S I W I L
Ꝗ Ɜ X ☉ W ☉ ▢ F ■ ▲ Ɔ ✦ ⊡ Δ A Δ B

L N O T G I V E Y O U M Y N A M E
▣ O T ● R u Ɔ ✛ ▢ ◔ Y ☉ ▢ ʌ S ☉ W

B E C A U S E Y O U W I   T O P M
V Z Ɜ G Y K E ▢ ⊤ Y A Δ   **L** ⌶ 𝝅 ☉

T O S L O I D O W N O R
H ⌶ F B X Δ ✦ X A D ◖ ╲   S L A V
       F ■ G Ɔ

Y C O L L E C T I N G O F
▢ Ɜ ◖ ▬ ▬ ◉ Ɜ ● P O R X ◖   I F E E
       P ◖ W ☉

E S F O R M Y A F T E R L
Z ◰ ⅃ T ⌶ ☉ ▢ ▲ ꓩ I ✛ ꓤ E   P I N
        𝙆 ⌶

B E O R I E T E M E T H
V E X ꓤ Δ W ⌶ ◉ ☉ E H ꓱ ◄ 𝝅 u

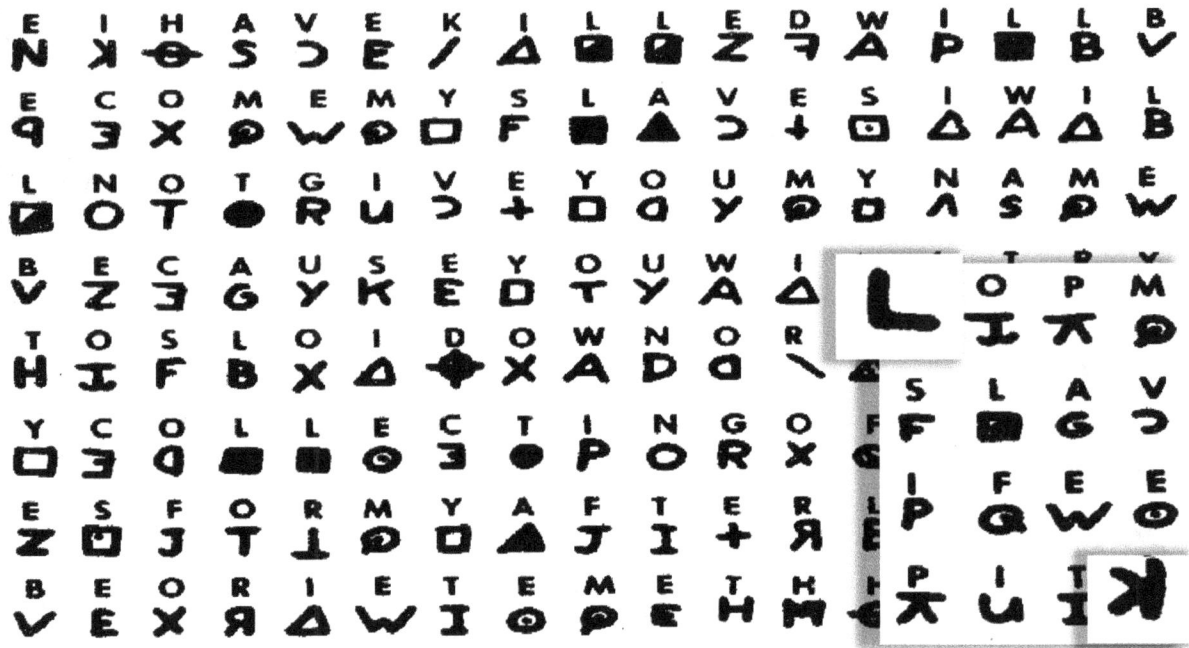

In the lower right corner is a 4-by-4 block. The characters in the upper left corner and in the lower right corner are the first and last characters in this block and they are the initials of the Zodiac. And they are facing each other—the L facing the right and the K facing the left—which gives us the Zodiac's initials of LARRY KLEIN/LARRY KANE/LARRY KAYE/LARRY KING.

L Ʞ

We can also find ZODIAC in each of the three ciphers. Here we see it in the "Vallejo Times Herald Cipher." The letters of ZODIAC are highlighted in this block. In fact, we find T-H-E Z-O-D-I-A-C. While investigators and journalists stated that he introduced his identity in a letter that was sent later, we see here that he actually first identified himself as the ZODIAC in his original cipher.

V E S M E T H E M O S T T H R I L
L I N G E X P E R E N C E I T I S
E V E N B E T T E R T H A N G E T
I I N G Y O U R R O C K S O F F W
I T H A G I R L T H E B E S T P A
R T O F I T I S T H A T W H E N I
D I E I W I L L B E R E B O R N I
N P A R A D I C E A N D A L L T H

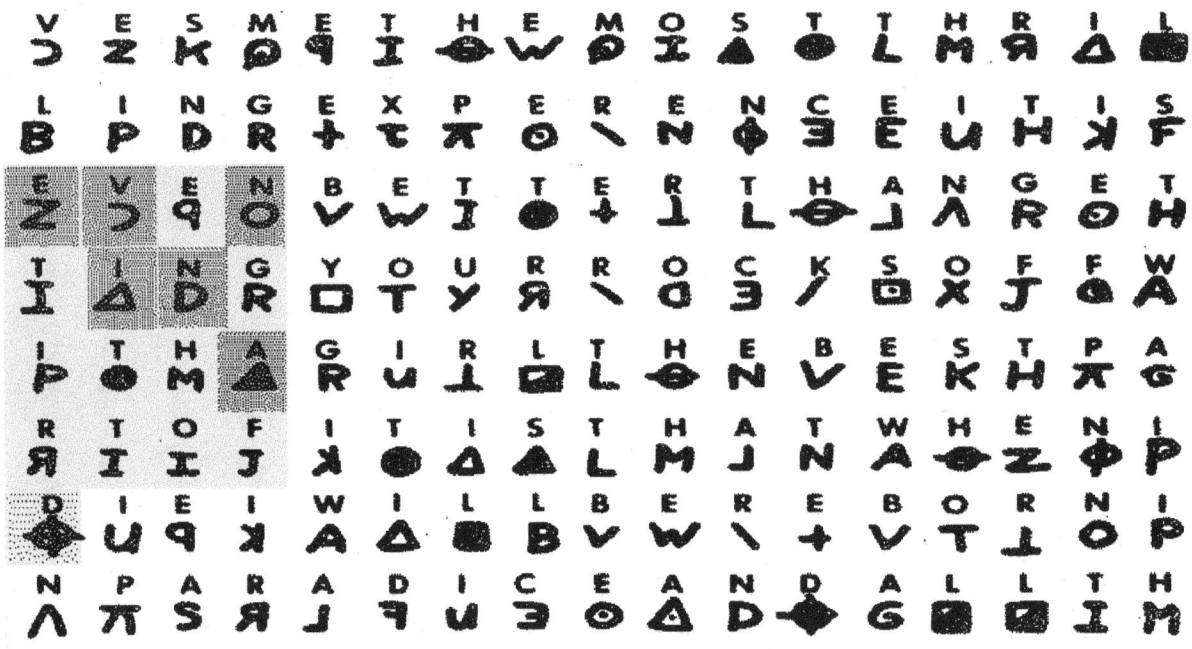

In the "Examiner Cipher," the Zodiac shares with us his alias again. And again, he calls himself T-H-E Z-O-D-I-A-C. We see T-H-E in this block along with Z-O-D-I-A-C. We also find that immediately below the block on the left is his Zodiac signature, the Circle Cross.

E I H A V E K I L L E D W I L L B
E C O M E M Y S L A V E S I W I L
L N O T G I V E Y O U M Y N A M E
B E C A U S E Y O U W I L L T R Y
T O S L O I D O W N O R S T O P M
Y C O L L E C T I N G O F S L A V
E S F O R M Y A F T E R L I F E E
B E O R I E T E M E T H H P I T I

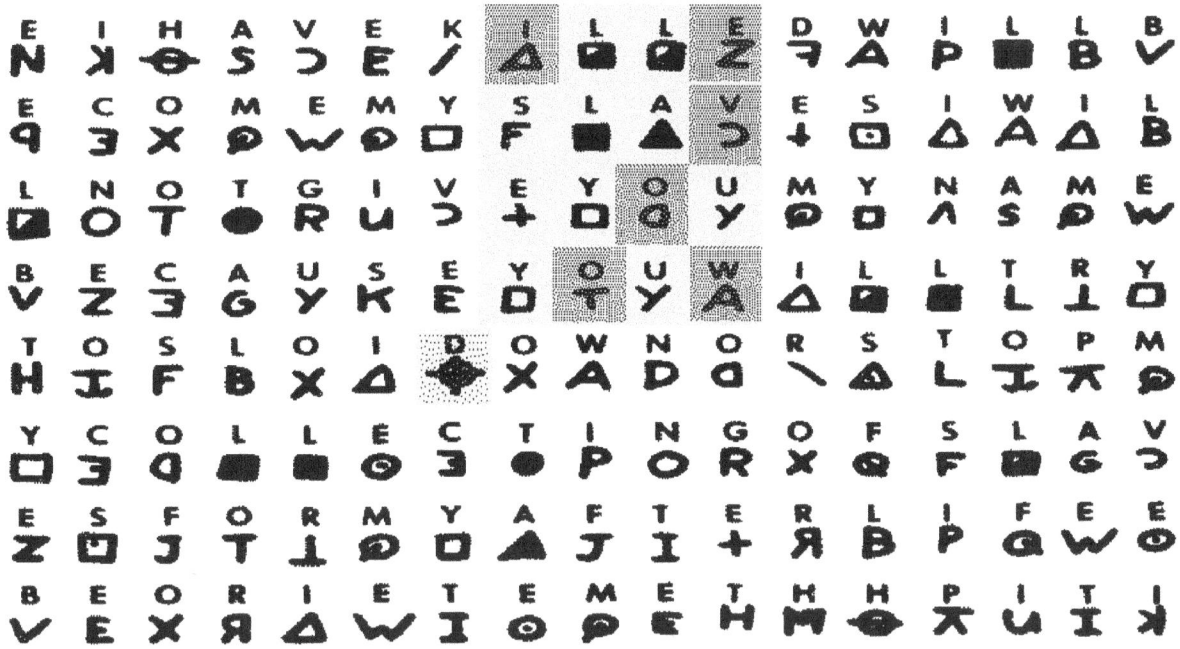

The Zodiac repeats this in the "Chronicle Cipher." He gives us Z-O-D-I-A-C. And in the block, we also see "I-L-L S-L-A-Y Y-O-U."

He signs it like he did the last one with his signature.

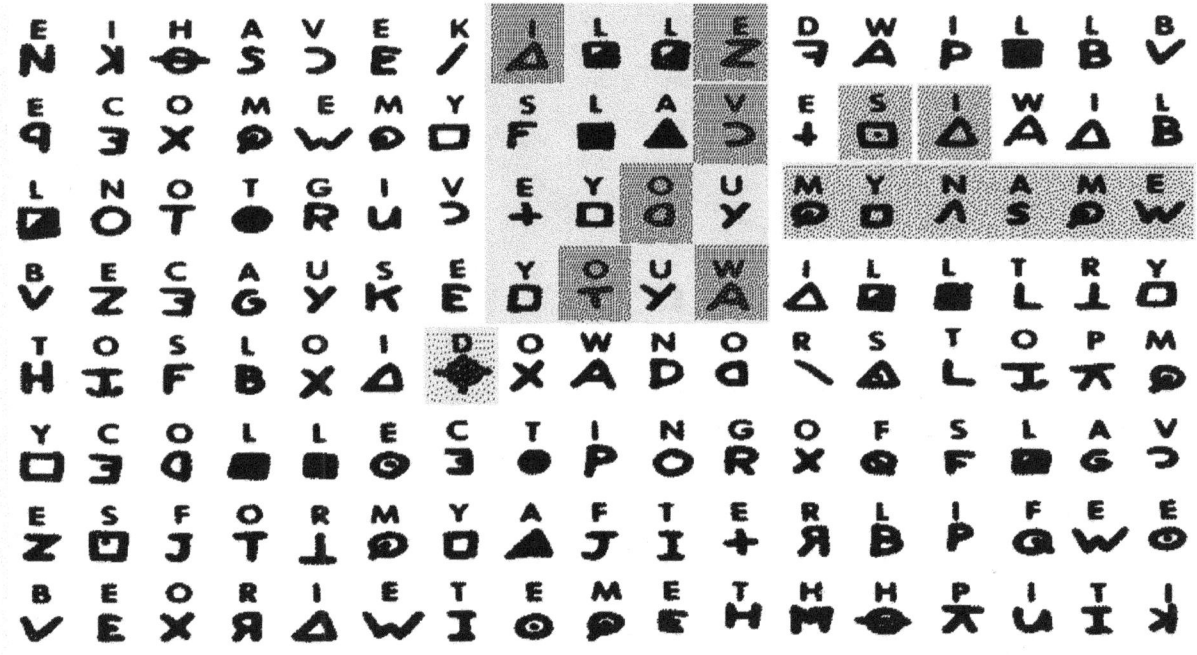

Cipher grid (letters annotated above each symbol):

```
E I H A V E K I L L E D W I L L B
E C O M E M Y S L A V E S I W I L
L N O T G I V E Y O U M Y N A M E
B E C A U S E Y O U W I L L T R Y
T O S L O I D O W N O R S T O P M
Y C O L L E C T I N G O F S L A V
E S F O R M Y A F T E R L I F E E
B E O R I E T E M E T H H P I I I
```

In the "Chronicle Cipher," we also find "Z-O-D-I-A-C I-S M-Y N-A-M-E."

As we have just seen, the Zodiac used 4-by-4 blocks to reveal his identity. Each of the three ciphers sent on July 31, 1969, displays the word ZODIAC in a 4-by-4 block. Two of them are signed with the Zodiac's Circle Cross signature.

In addition, in the "Times Herald Cipher" on page 120, the words "MY NAME" are seen just above and the word "IS" is seen just to the left of a 4-by-4 block in the lower right corner that gives us all four of the Zodiac's names with the initials LK —LARRY KANE/LARRY KLEIN/LAWRENCE KAY/LARRY KING. And in the "Chronicle Cipher" on page 158, in a 4-by-4 block, we find the Zodiac's initials—LK. The L is the first letter in the upper left corner of the block and the K is the last letter in the block in the lower right corner of the block. From this I determined the Zodiac was using 4-by-4 blocks and we can clearly see he manipulated letters in the blocks in order to reveal his identity. Moving from left to right, we see that letters that are needed to complete his name keep being replaced by letters in the next column.

When the three ciphers were sent to the three newspapers—the Vallejo Times Herald, the San Francisco Examiner, and the San Francisco Chronicle, the Zodiac stated in one of his accompanying letters, "Here is a cipher or that is part of one." This was his way of letting cryptographers believe either way. If cryptographers found the letter that begins, "I like killing people because it is so much fun…" they would be content that this is one cipher for the sake of one letter. And this is exactly what happened. When the ciphers were cracked by Bettye and Donald Harden, the three ciphers combined appeared to be one letter from the Zodiac, so it certainly appeared that the three ciphers were part of one cipher. And no one looked further.

For the sake of the letter found in the three ciphers, yes, it is one cipher. But beyond the letter and the taunting message found in the letter, which we know the Zodiac enjoyed immensely, we can see that this is no longer the case. Now we can see that the purpose of the letter was to give cryptographers something to crack. The larger purpose—indeed, the Zodiac's major purpose—was to reveal his identity. This would mean he would have to spread the letters in his names all over the ciphers so that his names or, often, both his first initial and one or more of his names would appear in numerous 4-by-4 blocks in as many places as possible in his three ciphers.

To accomplish this, he blended the Ciphertext with the Plaintext so they were both part of the Final Text. Between the Ciphertext and the Plaintext, he gives us multiple reveals of his four names that have the initials LK. The appearance of ZODIAC in each of the three ciphers also tells us they are three individual ciphers.

Furthermore, one cipher gives us "MY NAME IS LARRY KLEIN—MY NAME IS LARRY KANE—MY NAME IS LAWRENCE KAY—MY NAME IS LARRY KING"—in the lower right corner to end the first of the three ciphers.

Yes, he did enjoy taunting everyone, but his bigger purpose, we can see, was to reveal his identity.

And he did just that. The Zodiac revealed his identity in 4-by-4 blocks more than **200** times in the three ciphers—Z-136-A, Z-136-B, and Z-136-C.

We will see that in the Z-340 and Z-13 Ciphers, the texts are also blended. The letters from the Ciphertext are as much a part of the Final Text as the Plaintext.

THE

CIPHER

SENT TO THE

SAN FRANCISCO CHRONICLE

NOVEMBER 8, 1969

Z-340

BLENDED TEXT

The Zodiac didn't wait long after he had sent the first cipher, originally known as the Z-408, to send another cipher known as the Z-340. It was sent to the San Francisco Chronicle and was postmarked November 8, 1969.

I went right from examining the Z-408 to examining the Z-340. I knew right away that the Zodiac was using a Blended Text again.

The Z-340 Cipher was cracked in 2020 by David Oranchak, Sam Blake, and Jarl Van Eycke. The reason why it took so long to crack is because it was constructed in a very unusual way. It was in three parts and the first two parts were in a diagonal pattern. So, the original solution gives a Plaintext with Ciphertext that makes no sense unless we read one diagonal line at a time. This Plaintext with Ciphertext has been made available. Fortunately, a readable version has also been made available—one that can be read from left to right. So, there are two versions of the Z-340 and they are both examined in this book.

I have decided not to present all the appearances of the Zodiac's names in shaded 4-by-4 blocks like I did in the three ciphers known collectively as the Z-408. One reason is that it would be redundant. I have already shown you his purpose in sending ciphers. On the other hand, his names can be found in very small blocks or areas, sometimes smaller than 4-by-4 blocks.

There is something very interesting to note in the Z-340. Of the six least used letters in the English alphabet, five of the letters—Q, J, Z, X, and K—do not appear at all in the Plaintext*. There is nothing unusual about that at all. The Zodiac had no special purpose for three of the letters so he just put 3 'J's, 2 'Q's, and 2 'X's in the Ciphertext. He does put 4 'Z's in the Ciphertext so that he can put the word ZODIAC in both versions of the cipher.

What stands out and makes this very interesting is that the Zodiac went to the trouble of putting 12 'K's in the Ciphertext so that he could spread his names in the Final Text.

In deciphering the Z-340, I will reveal some very important clues that the Zodiac gave us at the bottom of the two versions of the cipher.

*It does appear that the Zodiac intended to have 1 K in the Plaintext to produce the word 'know' but instead he put the wrong characters and produced the word 'vnoe.'

Here is the original Z-340 Cipher as it was sent but with the Plaintext added. The message is diagonal and difficult to read.

I H O P E Y O U A R E H A V I N G
L O T S O F F A N I N T R Y I N G
T O C A T C H M E T H A T W A S N
T M E O N T H E T V S H O W W H I
C H B R I N G O U P A P O I N T A
B O U T M E I A M N O T A F R A I
D O F T H E G A S C H A M B E R B
E C A A S E I T W I L L S E N D M
E T O P A R A D L C E A L L T H E
S O O H E R B E C A U S E E N O W
H A V E E N O U G H S L A V E S T
O W O R A F O R M E W H E R E E V
E R Y O N E E L S E H A S N O T H
I N G W H E N T H E Y R E A C H P
A R A D I C E S O T H E Y A R E A
F R A I D O F D E A T H I A M N O
T A F R A I D B E C A U S E I V N
O E T H A T M Y N E W L I F E I S
L I F E W I L L B E A N E A S Y O
N E I N P A R A D I C E D E A T H

Here is the readable version of the Z-340 Final Text. This text is left to right and is easy to read.

I H O P E Y O U A R E H A V I N G
L O T S O F F A N I N T R Y I N G
T O C A T C H M E T H A T W A S N
T M E O N T H E T V S H O W W H I
C H B R I N G O U P A P O I N T A
B O U T M E I A M N O T A F R A I
D O F T H E G A S C H A M B E R B
E C A A S E I T W I L L S E N D M
E T O P A R A D L C E A L L T H E
S O O H E R B E C A U S E N O W
H A V E E N O U G H S L A V E S T
O W O R A F O R M E W H E R E E V
E R Y O N E E L S E H A S N O T H
I N G W H E N T H E Y R E A C H P
A R A D I C E S O T H E Y A R E A
F R A I D O F D E A T H I A M N O
T A F R A I D B E C A U S E I V N
O E T H A T M Y N E W L I F E I S
L I F E W I L L B E A N E A S Y O
N E I N P A R A D I C E D E A T H

"I'M T-H-E Z-O-D-I-A-C" can be found in the grey block.

L I F E W I L L B E A N E A S Y O

N E I N P A R A D I C E D E A T H

L I F E W I L L B E A N E A S Y O

N E I N P A R A D I C E D E A T H

Looking at the bottom two lines, we see the strongest and most obvious evidence of the Zodiac's intention to blend the two texts—the Ciphertext and the Plaintext.

L I F E W I L L B E A N E A S Y O

N E I N P A R A D I C E D E A T H

O Z A D I C

Each of the letters of ZODIAC can be found in a separate set. The first set in grey is a small A over a large O; the second set is an R over a Z, and so on. Using only one letter from each set, we find an anagram of ZODIAC.

L I F E W I L L B E A N E A S Y O

N E I N P A R A D I C E D E A T H

O Z A D I C
Z O D I A C

The appearance of ZODIAC in the near center of the bottom row of this version of the well-known Z-340 Cipher was placed there with a special purpose. There are six

172

consecutive sets—a set is defined as a large character from the Ciphertext and a smaller letter from the Plaintext above it. From the first set—an O and an A—we get the O; from the second set, we get the Z, from the third we get the A, from the fourth we get the D, from the fifth we get the I and from the sixth we get the C. The result is OZADIC which is an anagram of ZODIAC.

Also, notice that the Zodiac's Circle Cross signature substitutes for the A in ZODIAC and his last initial K stands for the I.

KLEIN　　　　　　　　**KANE/KAYE**　　**KAYE**

Here, we see a block with KLEIN, a block with KANE/KAYE, and another block with KAYE. What is noticeably noticeable and obviously obvious in the block with KANE/KAYE is that we see a K in the lower left corner and the other three letters of KANE are in consecutive letters--ANE. Or using the Y, we find the other three letters of KAYE in consecutive letters—AYE.

Z-O-D-I-A-C can be found in the grey block in this cipher as well.

174

Here we look at the bottom two lines of this version of the Z-340 and we find the same thing.

CI D A Z O

Again, we find an anagram of ZODIAC.

CI D A Z O

ZODIAC

ZODIAC is also in the near center of the bottom row of this version of the Z-340 Cipher, as well. This is also found in six consecutive sets—a set is defined as a large character from the Ciphertext and a smaller letter above it. From the first set—a backwards P and a C—we get the C, from the second set we get the I, from the third we get the D, from the fourth we get the A, from the fifth we get the Z and from the sixth we get the O. The result is CIDAZO which is an anagram of ZODIAC.

We see that the Zodiac has provided the letters in the word ZODIAC in six consecutive sets in order to convince us that this is all deliberate and on purpose.

Again, notice that the Zodiac's Circle Cross signature substitutes for the A in ZODIAC and his last initial K stands for the I.

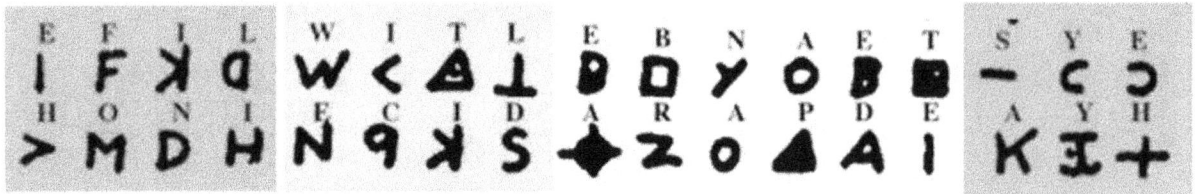

KLEIN   **KLEIN**   **KAYE**

At the bottom of this cipher, we find KLEIN in two small blocks, and KAYE in one block.

THE

Z-13

CIPHER

"MY

NAME

IS"

SENT TO THE

SAN FRANCISCO CHRONICLE

APRIL 20, 1970

BLENDED TEXT

The cipher known as the Z-13 was sent along with a bomb threat to the San Francisco Chronicle on April 20, 1970. I solved the Z-13 Cipher in 2021. In the letter we see "MY NAME IS" followed by this one-line cipher.

This is the Zodiac speaking

By the way have you cracked the last cipher I sent you?

My name is

A E N ⊕ ⊙ K ⊙ M ⊙ ⅃ N A M

I am mildly cerous as to how much money you have on my head now. I hope you do not think that I was the one who wiped out that blue meannie with a bomb at the cop station. Even though I talked about killing school children with one. It just wouldn't doo to move in on someone elses teritory. But there is more glory in killing a cop than a cid because a cop can shoot back. I have killed ten people to date. It would have been a lot more except that my bus bomb was a dud. I was swamped out by the rain we had a while back.

The new bomb is set up like this

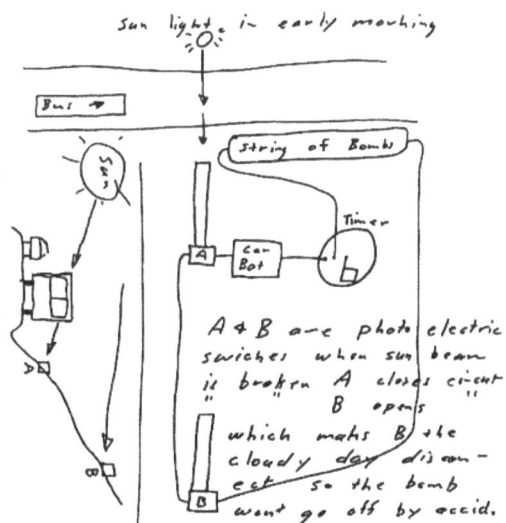

PS I hope you have fun trying to figgure out who I killed

⊕ =10   sfpd = 0

"MY NAME IS..."

A E N ⊕ ♉K♉M♉⚹ N A M

Knowing what we now know—that the Zodiac's ciphers are constructed so that (1) the Plaintext is a letter in order that a cryptologist can decipher it, (2) that there is a Final Text that is a blend of the letters in the Ciphertext and the letters in the Plaintext, and (3) the major purpose of the Final Text is to reveal the Zodiac's identity, we know exactly what he is doing in the Z-13. His only objective in the Z-13 is to give us his identity—nothing more—nothing less!

The Zodiac introduces the Z-13 with "MY NAME IS." He is telling us that he is about to give us his name. Up until now cryptologists have been unable to solve the Z-13 because they have assumed that the thirteen letters in the Plaintext will spell his name. Now that we know that the Zodiac reveals his name in a Final Text, we know that the Plaintext isn't his name. The Zodiac constructed the Ciphertext and the Plaintext using only the letters necessary to give us his identity. He tried to give us his identity in the Times Herald Cipher (page 120) where "MY NAME IS" leads us to his four names, but nobody got it. This time he wanted to make sure we got it, so this time there are just thirteen characters in the whole Z-13 Ciphertext—only eight of which are letters. The letters in the Ciphertext include an M followed by two non-alphabetical characters—either of which might substitute for a Y—followed by the first three letters of NAME. By all appearances, the Zodiac is giving us "MY NAME IS." The first four letters in the Ciphertext make an anagram of "KANE." Knowing that the Ciphertext is part of the Final Text, and already knowing our suspect, we have every reason to believe that he is giving us "MY NAME IS KANE."

This can only lead us to see that this is a repeat of what the Zodiac presented in the Times Herald Cipher. Again, he is giving us "MY NAME IS" followed by his names. In the Z-13, the eight letters in the Ciphertext—AEN-K-M-NAM—added to the thirteen letters in the up-until-now unsolved Plaintext will give us all the letters needed to spell "MY NAME IS LARRY KLEIN" and "MY NAME IS LARRY KANE" and "MY NAME IS LARRY KAYE" and "MY NAME IS LARRY KING."

The test is to see if this solution fills the requirements of the Final Text. We know that the three Taurus symbols ♉ must substitute for three of the same letter. This solution needs three of the letter Y for "MY" and "LARRY" and "KAYE." So, there is a match here. The Taurus symbols represent the letter Y.

There are also pairs of each of three letters in the Ciphertext. There are 2 'A's and 2 'M's and 2 'N's. Each of these pairs must substitute for another pair. It just so happens that this solution requires pairs of three letters. They are the I in "IS" and the I in "KLEIN/KING," the L in "LARRY" and the L in "KLEIN," and a pair of the letter R for the name, "LARRY." So, these are also a match.

Finally, there is one each of the characters, E, K, the Aries symbol ♈, and the Circle Cross ⊕.

These are congruent with the four other letters required to complete "MY NAME IS LARRY KLEIN/MY NAME IS LARRY KANE/MY NAME IS LARRY KAYE/MY NAME IS LARRY KING." These four single letters are the S in "IS," the other A that is needed for "KANE/KAYE," the other E that is needed for "KLEIN/KANE/KAYE," and the G that is needed for "KING."

So far—so good.

In addition to the letters in the Ciphertext we see here...

A E N ⊕ ♉ K ♉ M ♉ ♈ N A M

The other letters needed for the Final Text to spell "MY NAME IS" and his four names must be the following letters...

Y I S L R R Y L E I A Y G

These letters must, therefore, comprise the Plaintext. But to be a Plaintext the letters must make an actual sentence. Once we have a sentence, we will see what characters in the Ciphertext substitute for which letters in the Plaintext. Then we will have a Key. We will soon see if the letters can spell a sentence.

Let's see the Zodiac's mind at work as he constructed the Z-13...

A E N ⊕ ⊕ K ⊕ M ⊕ ⊥ N A M

The Zodiac has—in all of the other ciphers—given us a Ciphertext for which he expected us to solve the Key and produce a Plaintext. From a blend of the Ciphertext and the Plaintext, he expected us to find the Final Text which reveals his names. As we can see, this is not the case with the Z-13. In the Z-13, he wanted us to "see the obvious" and "know" the Final Text first. He expected us to know that the Final Text—the sum of all the letters in the Ciphertext and all the letters in the Plaintext—would give us all the letters necessary to spell each of the following...

MY NAME IS LARRY KLEIN
MY NAME IS LARRY KANE
MY NAME IS LARRY KAYE
MY NAME IS LARRY KING

The Final Text is the actual solution to the Z-13. Here are the letters in the Ciphertext we are given by the Zodiac. Note that unlike all the Zodiac's other ciphers, all the letters in the Ciphertext of the Z-13 are in their regular position in order to be perfectly clear...

A E N   K M   N A M

The remaining letters we need for the Final Text to reveal all of his names must be found in the Plaintext. The following are the letters in the Plaintext which must be unscrambled. The letters must make a sentence that makes sense.

Y I S L R R Y L E I A Y G

On top of all this, the Zodiac decided to use non-alphabetical symbols as he had done before...

⊕ had to be in the Ciphertext. All of his ciphers contain his signature.

His astrological sign would also be a great clue...

♉ After all, he was a Taurus. (The Taurus sign is circled to disguise it.)

He would eventually decide to make the Ciphertext symmetrical by using one more non-alphabetical symbol...

♈ is an inverted sign of Aries. He would complete this cipher and letter on the last of Aries—April 18 or 19. The letter was postmarked on April 20, 1970, which was a Monday. In 1970, Aries ended on April 20 at 12:14 PM. The Aries sign in the cipher would also make cryptographers look more closely at the Taurus sign. (The Aries sign is inverted to disguise it.)

The Zodiac now had to make a sentence out of these letters in order for there to be a Plaintext...

Y I S L R R Y L E I A Y G

Again, understand that these are the letters in the Plaintext. They must be unscrambled to find the Plaintext so that a Key to the cipher can be found.

I SLAY and GIRL

were right there.

Soon, he was relieved. He had figured it all out. A little awkward, but he was satisfied.

A E N ⊕ ⊗ K ⊗ M ⊙ ↧ N A M

I S L A Y E Y R Y G L I R

meaning...

I S L A Y E ' R Y G I R L

The Zodiac finally put together a Ciphertext and a Plaintext that made sense. As he saw this come together, he reflected on the fact that of his seven known attempts at murder as of April 1970, when he sent this cipher, two of his victims had survived. They were both males. But he had killed every girl that he had tried to kill. So, he put together a sentence that made sense. "I SLAY EVERY GIRL" But there was no V—just another Y. So, he used "EYRY."

The first thing we must consider is that he misspelled words in all of his letters and ciphers. Secondly, the top part of the Y does form a V. But it is also important for us to consider that EYRY is actually also a word. It is a word for 'a nest made by birds of prey.' It is not known if Larry Kane was aware of this word, but he did treat humans as birds of prey. It is also quite possible or even probable that he looked up E'RY or already knew that E'RY is used as a poetic contraction of EVERY and as an eye-dialect spelling of EVERY. Another error was his misspelling of "GIRL." It appears that it was more important to the Zodiac to give away "NAME" in the Ciphertext with "NAM" than it was to spell "GIRL" correctly.

The letters in the Ciphertext—AEN—K-M—NAM—added to the thirteen letters in the Plaintext—I SLAY EYRY GIRL—add up to the twenty-one (21) letters in the Final Text which are the letters in...

MY NAME IS LARRY KLEIN/A/Y/G

The A is needed for KANE, the Y is for KAYE, and the G is for KING.

THE KEY TO THE Z-13

ՆՆՆ	——	YYY
AA	——	II
NN	——	LL
MM	——	RR
E	——	S
K	——	E
ᚱ	——	G
⊕	——	A

A E N ⊕ ՆKՆMՆᚱ N A M

I SL A YEYR YGLIR

I SL A YE'RY GIRL

Having unscrambled the Plaintext from the other letters necessary to spell out "MY NAME IS" and the Zodiac's names, we now have a Key to the Z-13.

In summary, the Ciphertext A-E-N-K-M-N-A-M added to the Plaintext I-S-L-A-Y-E-Y-R-Y-G-I-R-L gives us all the letters necessary and, in fact, only the letters necessary for us to spell each of the following...

MY NAME IS LARRY KLEIN
MY NAME IS LARRY KANE
MY NAME IS LARRY KAYE
MY NAME IS LARRY KING

Once again, this is the Final Text and this is the solution to the Z-13.

The Zodiac would have believed that law enforcement could solve the Z-408, Z-340, and the Z-13 Ciphers because he assumed they knew his four names with the initials—LK—from his arrest records.

The following arrest record confirms that LAWRENCE KLEIN/LARRY KLEIN was arrested under the names LAWRENCE KLEIN, LAWRENCE KAYE, and LAWRENCE KANE before the Zodiac Killer sent the ciphers.

Another arrest that is on record—an arrest in Louisiana—confirms that LAWRENCE KAYE committed adultery while using the alias LARRY KING.

He was not arrested as LAWRENCE CANE until long after the period of time the Zodiac sent the ciphers. It appears to this author that his change to the name LAWRENCE CANE strongly suggests that he no longer wanted to be arrested for the murders of the Zodiac Killer. He knew that the displays of his initials LK twice and his surname KANE appearing many times in his ciphers would increase his chances of getting caught. His name change, his new pride in his career in sales and real estate, and his change in the direction of his life required that he have a name change.

UNITED STATES DEPARTMENT OF JUSTICE
FEDERAL BUREAU OF INVESTIGATION
WASHINGTON 25 D.C.

Police Dept Los Angeles, CA	Larry Kaye	10/18/46	Battery 2 counts
Sheriff Office Hackensack, NJ	Lawrence Klein	9/22/47	Conspiracy to Defraud
Police Dept New York, NY	Lawrence Kaye	6/16/52	Burglary
Probation Dept Court of General Sessions New York, NY	Larry Kaye	6/16/52	Burglary
Police Dept Hattiesburg, Miss	Lawrence Kaye	9/5/59	Disturbance of of the Peace
Police Dept Alameda, CA	Lawrence Kane	9/10/61	Peaking in Window
Police Dept Palo Alto, CA	Larry Kane	12/3/63	Shoplifting
Sheriff Office Oak Brook, Il	Larry Kane	9/5/64	Shoplifting

This arrest record of LAWRENCE KLEIN/ KANE/KAYE is reprinted in order to be in readable form.

UNITED STATES DEPARTMENT OF JUSTICE
FEDERAL BUREAU OF INVESTIGATION
WASHINGTON 25 D.C.

Sheriff's Office Wheaton, Il	Larry Kane	9/5/64	Theft
Police Dept Menlo Park, CA	Lawrence Klein	3/27/65	Petty Theft
Police Dept Miami Beach, FL	Lawrence Kane	7/11/66	Illegal Use of Credit Card
Police Dept Redwood City, CA	Lawrence Kane	8/29/68	Prowling
Police Dept Placerville, CA	Lawrence Cane	10/1/80	Theft of Personal Property

KANE was also arrested in Algiers, Louisiana in 1960 for adultery. He was arrested under the name LAWRENCE KAYE, but the name he was using at the time was LARRY KING.

As we can see, he was arrested under the names LAWRENCE KLEIN/LAWRENCE KAYE/LAWRENCE KANE.

THE ZODIAC'S ZODIAC

A E N ⊕ ♉ ♉ K ♉ M ♉ ♈ N A M

The three identical symbols are Taurus symbols. The tenth symbol is an Aries symbol. As the letter was written and mailed on April 19—the last day of Aries—we can make an educated guess that the Zodiac used the Aries sign to tell us when he wrote it and to bring more attention to the three identical symbols so we might notice that they are encircled Taurus symbols. In a symmetrical fashion, he signs the Cipher with his crosshairs sign four symbols from the left and dates it four symbols from the right. In the very middle with symmetry as well are the three Taurus signs.

My work with the Zodiac ciphers had led to my discovery that the Zodiac Killer had blended the Plaintext with the characters in the Ciphertext that were actually letters of the alphabet to form a Final Blended Text. The Big Reveal is that he was LAWRENCE KLEIN/KANE/KAYE/KING. There was already no question in my mind.

You can never have too much evidence, however, and I wanted my work with the Zodiac Killer to be complete. Calling himself the Zodiac implied some kind of connection to astrology. So, I thought I would now hunt for astrological signs and clues in his ciphers and pictures and the many letters he had written. There were some astrological symbols among the characters in the ciphers and a lot of drawings that came with his letters.

I enlarged the ciphers in order to get a better look. I found that three identical characters in the Z-13 Cipher—the cipher that follows "MY NAME IS..."—were actually Taurus symbols inside a circle. Another symbol in the same cipher could be interpreted as an inverted (upside-down) symbol of Aries.

The three Taurus symbols identify the Zodiac Killer as a Taurus. This would be the killer's own reveal that he was born between April 20 and May 19. The Aries symbol could only communicate to us that the letter was written on April 17 or April 18. After all, the letter was received on April 20, 1970, which was a Monday. They don't deliver mail on Sunday.

I made a list of all of the major Zodiac Killer suspects. Then I added other names to the list. These were names of men who had become a popular subject of public speculation. A couple of suspects were men whose own son believed them to be the infamous serial killer.

I would argue that not only was the Zodiac Killer "maybe," "perhaps," "most likely" a Taurus—the Zodiac Killer was "in fact," "most certainly," "without a doubt" a Taurus! As I completed the list and looked it over, I saw that one suspect is a Taurus.

The following is a list of the many suspects from law enforcement and from the public that includes their birthday and astrological sign.

ARTHUR LEIGH ALLEN/ "LEE"
DECEMBER 18, 1933
SAGITARIUS

ROSS MARIO SULLIVAN
JULY 28, 1941
LEO

JOHN WALKER TARRANCE / "JACK"
FEBRUARY 24, 1928
PISCES

RICHARD JOSEPH GAIKOWSKI / "DICK GIKE"
MARCH 14, 1936
PISCES

ROBERT IVAN NICHOLS
SEPTEMBER 12, 1926
VIRGO

EDWARD WAYNE EDWARDS
JUNE 14, 1932
GEMINI

EARL VAN BEST
JULY 14, 1934
CANCER

GEORGE HILL HODEL
OCTOBER 10, 1907
LIBRA

GARY FRANCIS POSTE
NOVEMBER 8, 1937
SCORPIO

LOUIS JOSEPH MYERS
JANUARY 10, 1952
CAPRICORN

PAUL ALFRED DOERR
APRIL 1, 1927
ARIES

BRUCE MCGREGOR DAVIS
OCTOBER 5, 1942
LIBRA

FRANK ROBERT DRYMAN
JUNE 4, 1931
GEMINI

ʊ ʊ ʊ

LAWRENCE KLEIN/KANE/KAYE/KING
APRIL 29, 1924
TAURUS

To summarize what we have just seen, the Z-13 Cipher has revealed that the Zodiac was a Taurus, and there is only one Taurus among the most popular suspects of law enforcement and the public.

The Zodiac, as we know, was born LARRY KLEIN on April 29, 1924, making him a Taurus.

THE ZODIAC WATCH

One thing that was noticed by those who wore a Zodiac watch or who saw ads for the Zodiac watch was that the serial killer who called himself the Zodiac used the Zodiac name and the Zodiac watch Circle Cross logo as his signature. In fact, he includes his Zodiac signature in all of his ciphers and in every letter that was not anonymous. He also calls himself Zodiac in all of his ciphers except for the Z-13.

The question we will likely never get answered is why he chose to call himself the Zodiac and why he used the Zodiac watch logo. Did he first decide to call himself the Zodiac and then see the ads and adopt the logo? Did he like the Circle Cross symbol first and then see the ads? Or did he choose the name Zodiac and the logo at the same time?

One possibility I will introduce is that he read Jack London's 1904 novel *The Sea Wolf* and/or watched a film version of *The Sea Wolf*. According to this theory, he identified with the story's narcissistic and psychopathic character—Wolf Larsen. Seeing the Zodiac diver's watch called the Sea Wolf, that first came out in 1953, inspired him to call himself the Zodiac and use the logo as his signature. This theory does get some support from the possibility that his mention of "Man is the most dangerous animal" in his Z-408 cipher might be a reference to *The Most Dangerous Game*—the 1924 short story by Richard Connell—that also became a movie in which the antagonist is a narcissistic psychopath.

We are learning who Larry Kane was. If he was the kind of person who would read or watch *The Most Dangerous Game*, he could very well be the same kind of person who would read or watch *The Sea Wolf*. They both have an antagonist who is a cruel narcissistic psychopath. If Kane identified with Zaroff from *The Most Dangerous Game*, he might also identify with Wolf Larsen or vice versa.

Another possibility is that he liked the logo because it resembled the cross hairs of guns and targets. With the logo came the name "Zodiac" when he saw them together.

One more theory worth mentioning is that he followed the Zodiac—meaning astrology. He does give us his Zodiac sign and he does give us the Zodiac sign of the day he wrote the Z-13 Cipher. He also mentions someone's Zodiac sign in a letter he wrote long before the murders.

It is interesting to note that the Zodiac watch Circle Cross logo resembles the Irish Celtic Cross which is a Christian cross that first appeared in the ninth century in Ireland, Britain, and France. The possibility of the Zodiac being attracted to the Celtic Cross is not likely as he was neither Irish, British or French, and he wasn't Christian. He was raised Jewish.

The one thing that we can assume is that the Zodiac was aware of the Zodiac watch and the logo.

THE CITIZEN CLUE

August 10, 1969
San Francisco, California

Dear Sergeant Lynch,

I hope the enclosed "key" will prove to be beneficial to you in connection with the cipher letter writer.
Working puzzles criptograms and word puzzle is one of my pleasure. Please forgive the absence of my signature or name as I do not wish to have my name in the papers and it could be mentioned at the slip of the tongue

With best wishes,
Concerned citizen

On August 10, 1969, Detective John Lynch received a letter from a "Concerned Citizen." The letter was not published in any of the newspapers. So, the 'Citizen' typed another letter (postmarked October 7, 1969) which he also sent to John Lynch. It was signed "Good Citizen." The two "Citizen" letters were not published, and they were never very well-known to the public. Many doubted these two letters were the work of the Zodiac Killer.

May 8, 1974
San Francisco, California

Sirs- I would like to express my consternation concerning your poor taste & lack of sympathy for the public, as evidenced by your running of the ads for the movie "Badlands," featuring the blurb - "In 1959 most people were killing time. Kit & Holly were killing people." In light of recent events, this kind of murder-glorification can only be deplorable at best (not that glorification of violence was ever justifiable) why don't you show some concern for public sensibilities & cut the ad?

A citizen

Then, on May 8, 1974, he sent his third "Citizen" letter on a card. The Zodiac never sent a letter without a purpose. The three citizen letters—"Concerned Citizen"—"Good Citizen"—"A Citizen"—give us a big clue about one of the Zodiac's aliases. One of the biggest films ever—a movie starring Orson Welles—sometimes considered the best movie of all time is...

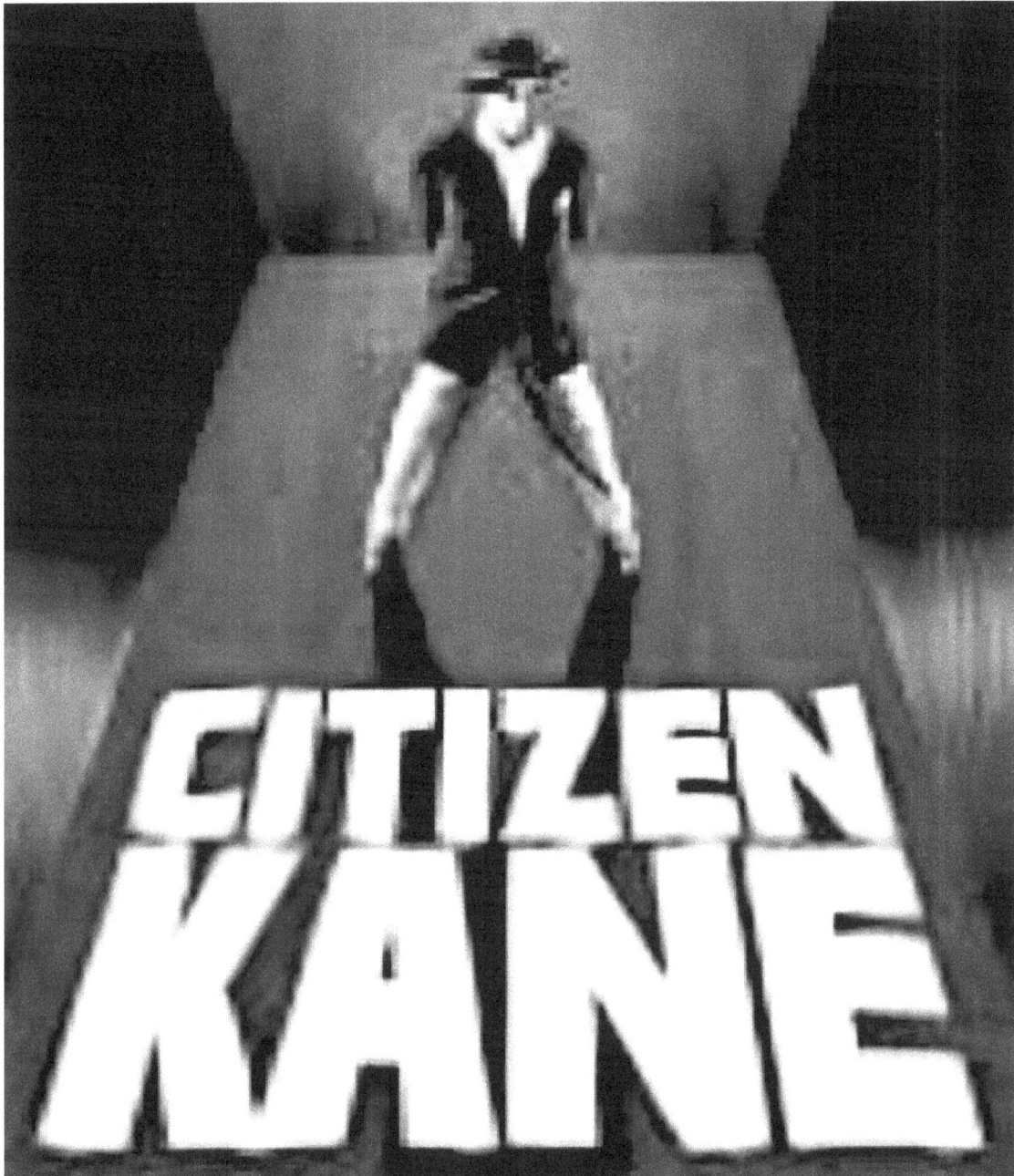

Larry Kane was 17 when CITIZEN KANE hit the theatres. The movie was still well-known and highly regarded when he wrote the first two "Citizen" letters in 1969 and when he wrote the third one in 1974.

We can see that the three "Citizen" letters were a clue which revealed the Zodiac's identity. And the three letters have the most famous word 'CITIZEN' in a movie and that movie is CITIZEN KANE. This clue leads us to the suspect LARRY KANE.

THE HERB CAEN CLUE

April 24, 1978
San Francisco, California

Dear Editor

This is the Zodiac speaking, I am back with you. Tell herb Caen I am here. I have always been here. That city pig Toschi is good - but I am smarter and better he will get tired then leave me alone. I am waiting for a good movie about me. who will play me? I am now in control of all things.

Yours truly:

⊕ - guess

SFPD - 0

Even in 1978, the Zodiac was still trying to give away his identity. In fact, this letter that he sent to the editor of the San Francisco Chronicle was more than a clue. In the letter, the Zodiac mentions Herb Caen who was a journalist and humorist for the Chronicle. Caen had written an article on fellow journalist Paul Avery who requested a personalized license plate that would say "ZODIAC." Of the many journalists and police officers the Zodiac could have mentioned, his choice was Herb Caen. And he is asking the editor of the paper to "Tell herb Caen I am here." He didn't say, "Leave him a note." He said, "Tell him." If the editor knew the Zodiac by name, he would be telling Herb Caen that Larry Kane was here. Although they are spelled differently, the two names are pronounced the same way. So, the Zodiac was giving us the clue that his name was KANE.

ALL GOOD CHILDREN
GO TO HEAVEN

May 2, 1978
Hollywood, California

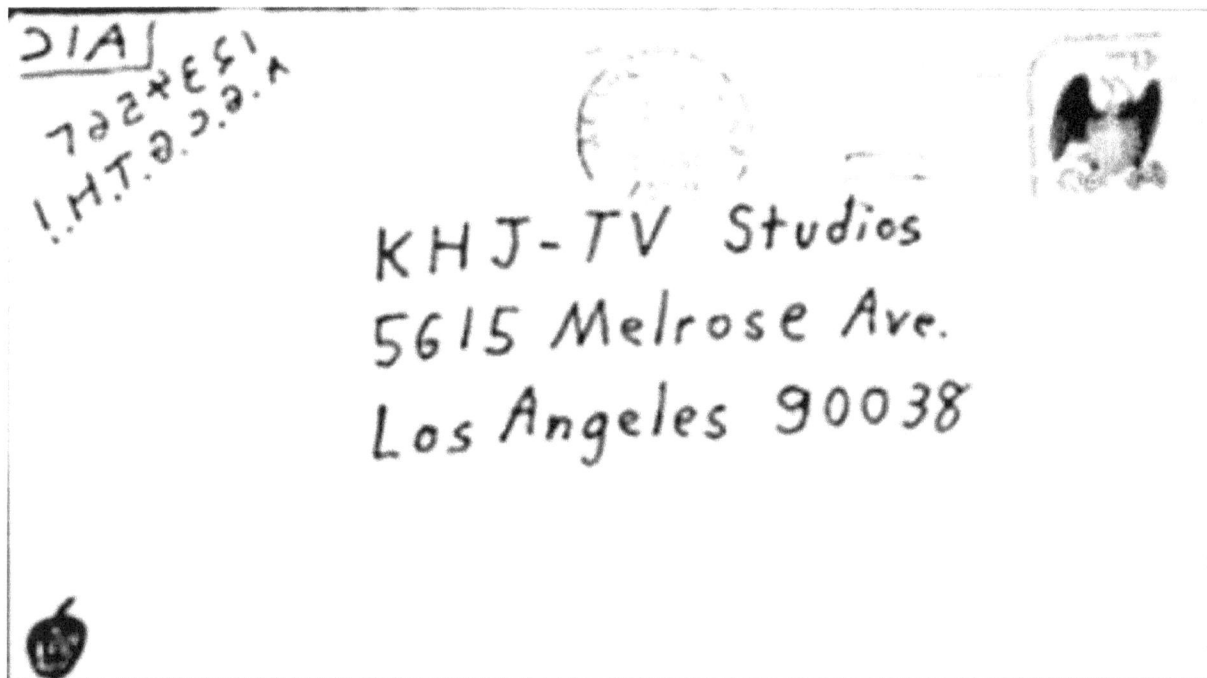

On May 2, 1978, a letter was sent to KHJ-TV Studios in Hollywood, California. The envelope contained a clue in the upper left corner. 7654321 HTGCGA. Backwards, this is 1234567 AGCGTH. AGCGTH stands for "All Good Children Go To Heaven." In the Beatles song *You Never Give Me Your Money*, the Beatles sing "1-2-3-4-5-6-7 All Good Children Go To Heaven."

Everything the Zodiac sent contained a clue—either in a letter, in a cipher, or on an envelope. The Zodiac never wasted a letter.

In fact, he draws the Apple representing the logo of the Beatles record label in the lower left corner of the envelope as a further hint that this is the Beatles song he is referring to with the old children's rhyme.

But first things first. The song was written by Paul McCartney and it had an important meaning to him. The Beatles had a practice of saying things to people in their songs. For example, John Lennon expressed his feelings about the Maharishi Mahesh Yogi in the Beatles song *Sexy Sadie*. After the break-up of the band, John, George, and Ringo wrote songs to Paul and Paul wrote songs to them.

Paul wrote some of the *You Never Give Me Your Money* medley to express his thoughts and feelings and his upsets about their manager, ALLEN KLEIN.

Yes, the manager's first name was ALLEN which was the surname of one of the major suspects—ARTHUR LEIGH ALLEN. And KLEIN is the surname he shares with our suspect—LARRY KLEIN.

LARRY KLEIN was giving us his last name by giving us a reference to ALLEN KLEIN.

I may have considered this a hint that the Zodiac could be either ARTHUR LEIGH ALLEN or LAWRENCE KLEIN.

BUT NOW WE KNOW!

THE
ZODIAC
KILLER

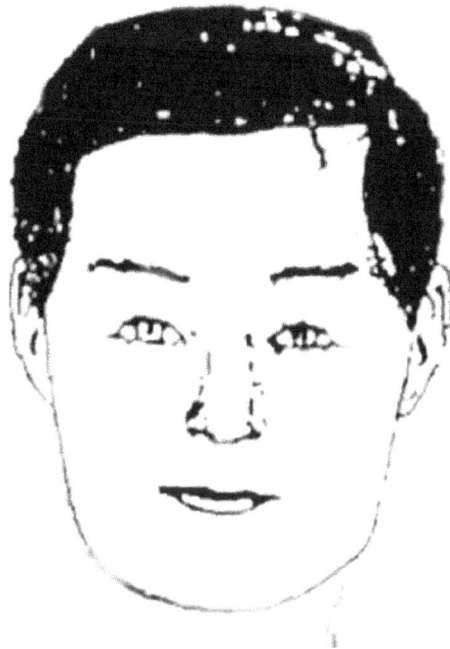

LAWRENCE KLEIN/KANE/KAYE/KING/CANE/THE ZODIAC KILLER

(April 29, 1924 - May 10, 2010)

LAWRENCE KANE, born LAWRENCE KLEIN (April 29, 1924 - May 10, 2010) was an American serial killer and career criminal. He is better known as the Zodiac or as the Zodiac Killer. In the late 1960s and early 1970s, he terrorized Northern California with cold-blooded murders and through the taunting of the public, the police, and the press with a series of letters and ciphers. The Zodiac case was considered to be the most famous unsolved murder case in U.S. history until the Zodiac was identified by David Daniel in 2023.

Five murders have been absolutely attributed to him by a consensus of the authorities, but many more suspected victims have been connected to him by other law enforcement and/or the media and/or family members and/or others. In one of his communications, Kane, himself, claimed to have murdered 37 people.

Now that his identity has been established, investigators may be able to narrow down a list of his most likely victims.

Childhood

Lawrence Klein was born April 29, 1924, in Brooklyn, New York to Morris Heim "Harry" Klein and Sarah Benjamin. Both parents were of Jewish heritage. His father was from Hungary and his mother's parents were from Russia. They had two other children, but neither of them survived infancy.

His parents divorced when he was thirteen. He was raised by his mother. They formed an unnatural, psychological dependence on each other.

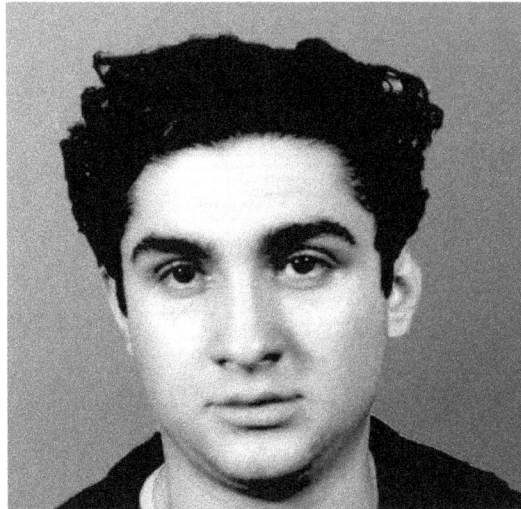

Early Adulthood

One of his earliest jobs was being a master of ceremonies at nightclubs—a job he very much enjoyed. As an emcee, he had the undivided attention of the audience.

He also began dating singers who he met as an emcee.

On September 13, 1941, Klein, then aged 17, changed his name through the Social Security Administration to Lawrence Kaye, stating it would be "beneficial for employment in my field." His name change may have been due to the strong antisemitism of the day. His name change could also have been influenced by the idea that if he used a show business-sounding name, it would be advantageous to him. Two celebrities who were big at the time were Sammy Kaye and Danny Kaye. (In fact, Danny Kaye was Jewish and had changed his surname from Kaminsky). He would eventually take on other aliases, two of them also with the same initials—

LK. These were Lawrence Kane and Lawrence King. He was primarily identifying himself as Lawrence Kane at the time of the Zodiac murders.

He enlisted in the Navy as Lawrence Klein on February 12, 1943. He was accepted into the Electronics Training Program. To be accepted into that program, he had to pass the Eddy test which showed that he had a high aptitude.

He was discharged from the Navy on September 23, 1943, after serving just a little over seven months, with an honorable discharge based on a diagnosis of "psychoneurosis hysteria." This was reported to be related to his pathological relationship with his mentally unstable and chronically ill mother.

After his brief stint in the Navy, he went back to using the name Larry Kaye and he returned to show business as a master of ceremonies. He was romantically linked in newspapers to a number of singers, including Denise Darcel and Dory Previn.

He was married three times. On July 7, 1945, he married his first wife, Eileen Phyllis Barton—a singer who appeared on Frank Sinatra's radio show. She had a number of hits, including "If I Knew You Were Coming I'd've Baked a Cake—which was number one on *Billboard's Most Played by Jockeys* for ten weeks. He had two more wives named Cynthia Brooks (February 13, 1954) and Ethel Marie Brown (December 30, 1959). His divorce from his third wife was due to his adultery, for which he had been arrested. In fact, all three of his marriages were brief and ended in divorce.

Early Criminal History

He began his life as a career criminal quite early. He was first arrested in 1941 at the age of 17. His arrests continued through the 1940s, 1950s, and 1960s under several names, including Lawrence Klein, Lawrence Kaye, and Lawrence Kane, and he was using the name Lawrence King while committing adultery for which he was arrested. His record includes larceny, conspiracy, burglary, peeping in windows, and prowling.

His arrests not only went on his record. Many of his arrests were in newspapers. The story of the arrests, the outcomes of the arrests, and the charges being filed or dropped were often stories in the papers. Some of these events were not listed on his record.

Auto Collision

He had a serious auto collision in 1962. This was said to have caused severe brain damage. In 1965, an evaluation said his rehabilitation from the collision was poor. He was also said to be losing his ability to control self-gratification and he began to have seizures.

Arrest for Prowling

Now using the name Kane, he was arrested in 1961 for peeping in windows. This appears to be his first arrest for a crime that was of a sexual nature.

Kane was arrested in Redwood City, California on August 29, 1968, for prowling. This was just four months before his first known murder on December 20, 1968. This event may have had some significance. He may have been prowling for victims.

The Zodiac Murders

At least by December 20, 1968, Larry Kane began committing murder. His first known victims were couples who were sitting in their car, parked for the purpose of romance. His last known victim was a lone male taxi driver. Five of seven people he attempted to murder died, the other two, both males, survived. These attacks took place in the San Francisco Bay Area.

He shot and killed David Arthur Faraday, 17, and Betty Lou Jensen, 16, on December 20, 1968, on a road known as a Lovers Lane. He shot Michael Renault Mageau, 19, and Darlene Elizabeth Ferrin, 22, on July 4, 1969, in the parking lot of a park. Michael Mageau survived. Kane stabbed Bryan Calvin Hartnell, 20, and Cecelia Ann Shepard, 22, on September 27, 1969, at Lake Berryessa in Napa County. Cecelia Shepard died two days later; Bryan Hartnell survived.

His seventh victim—his fifth fatal victim—was a lone male taxi driver, Paul Stine, 29, who he shot on October 11, 1969. It is suspected that he killed Stine because he believed that Stine knew where he lived or that he might know too much.

Letters and Ciphers

Lawrence Kane's first known letters and ciphers were sent July 31, 1969, to three newspapers—the Vallejo Times Herald, the San Francisco Examiner, and the San Francisco Chronicle. One of the accompanying letters stated that the cipher reveals his identity. In less than a week, a couple named Bettye and Donald Harden were able to decipher a letter from the three ciphers. This gave the ciphers an order. The "Times Herald Cipher" was to be studied first, then the "Examiner Cipher" and then the "Chronicle Cipher." The combined cipher is known as the Z-408. Daniel refers to the three ciphers separately as the Z-136-A, Z-136-B, and Z-136-C. On July 11, 2021, Daniel further cracked the three ciphers—revealing the Zodiac's surnames multiple times. Each of the ciphers also reveals the word ZODIAC and contains the Zodiac's signature.

Since no one found the word ZODIAC in the ciphers, the Zodiac wrote a letter that begins, "This is the Zodiac speaking…"

He then sent more ciphers. The cipher known as the Z-340 also reveals the word ZODIAC and his many surnames. The Z-13 was a follow-up to the Z-136-A—the "Vallejo Times Herald Cipher." He states "MY NAME IS…" and gives us all of his names with the initials LK—LARRY KLEIN/LARRY KANE/LARRY KAYE/LARRY KING.

Larry Kane continued to send letters, cards, and ciphers up until 1978. There may have been a clue with everything he sent. It may have been in a cipher, in a letter, on a card, or on an envelope. He seldom—if ever—sent anyone anything without there being a purpose.

The Zodiac Name and Signature

Long before Larry Kane began to murder and send ciphers and letters identifying himself as the Zodiac, there was a watchmaker company called ZODIAC, and the ZODIAC brand used the Circle Cross symbol as its logo on its watches. The reason Larry Kane used the name ZODIAC and the logo of the watch will likely never be known with certainty.

Later Adulthood and Death

Larry Kane began to use the name Larry Cane by 1980, perhaps to distance himself from the initials LK. No longer wanting to be a suspect in the Zodiac murders and living a different life may have been the cause of this change.

His new life included work in real estate and in sales. He likely read books and magazine articles about the Zodiac, and he likely saw the films about the Zodiac and films that were inspired by the Zodiac.

LARRY CANE/LARRY KANE/LARRY KING/LARRY KAYE/LARRY KLEIN died in Reno, Nevada at the age of 86. He died a suspect in the Zodiac killings—wondering but never knowing if his identity would ever be revealed.

Discovery of the Zodiac's Identity

On July 11, 2021, David Daniel discovered the identity of the Zodiac Killer. He further deciphered the Z-408, which he refers to as the Z-136-A, Z-136-B, and Z-136-C and further deciphered the Z-340. He fully deciphered the Z-13. He also solved a number of clues left by the Zodiac. David Daniel published his results in 2023.

The discovery of the Zodiac's identity means that law enforcement can now study one man—one individual. His footsteps can be traced through the locations of his work and the locations of his arrests. Old interviews with witnesses that link Larry Kane to victims or suspected victims can assist law enforcement in establishing or confirming connections between Kane and likely victims.

Larry Kane's psychological history can be examined more closely and it may be possible to connect this history with his progression from a psychopathic career criminal to the notorious serial killer that we call the Zodiac Killer.